A-78

THE COMPLETE
BEGINNER'S GUIDE TO
SOARING AND
HANG GLIDING

THE COMPLETE BEGINNER'S GUIDE TO

SOARING AND HANG GLIDING

Norman Richards

DOUBLEDAY & COMPANY, INC.

GARDEN CITY, NEW YORK

PHOTO CREDITS:

Julie Evans, p. 47
Flexi Flier, p. 77
Sheridan Jackson, Manta Wings, pp. 80, 93
Manta Wings, p. 103
Norman Richards, p. 76
Schweizer Aircraft Corporation, pp. 3, 9, 14, 16, 39, 50, 52
Russ Thompson, Manta Wings, p. 66
Volmer Aircraft, pp. 84, 85
John F. Wellsman, Man-Flight Systems Inc., pp. 68, 82, 86, 94, 100, 102

Soaring artwork by Barbara E. Mills
Hang gliding artwork by John Kennedy

Library of Congress Cataloging in Publication Data

Richards, Norman.
  The complete beginner's guide to soaring and
hang gliding.

    Includes index.
    SUMMARY: A guide to soaring and hang gliding
including getting started, flying the aircraft, and
the aerodynamic principles involved in each sport.
    1. Gliding and soaring—Juvenile literature.
[1. Gliding] I. Title.
GV764.R5   797.5'5
ISBN 0-385-05155-7 Trade
      0-385-08318-1 Prebound
Library of Congress Catalog Card Number 74–18827

For my parents

Acknowledgments

I would like to thank a talented lady, Barbara E. Mills, for contributing her fine illustrations on soaring. I'm equally grateful to John Kennedy, artist and skilled hang glider pilot, for his instructional drawings on that sport. Thanks also to Mike Markowski and Bob Goodness of Man-Flight Systems for their hang gliding photographs and advice. I'm grateful to the Soaring Society of America and the U. S. Hang Gliding Association for their information; the manufacturers of sailplanes and hang gliders for photos and drawings; and Richard "Old Dog" Wolters, author of *The Art and Technique of Soaring*, who kindled my enthusiasm for the sport when I first met him several years ago.

Contents

PART I

SOARING

1

Getting Started

The Why and How of Soaring

What worlds are left to conquer in aviation? It can be discouraging for the typical pilot seeking adventure and challenge. The men and women who grew up with aviation in the twenties and thirties—the barnstormers, the air racers, and the solo long-distance record setters—have seen technological progress sweep their individual achievements aside. Sleek, multi-million-dollar jet planes have broken the sound barrier, flown over every remote corner of the world, and set speed, distance, and altitude records beyond the wildest dreams of traditional aviators. It has become big business, requiring teamwork rather than adventurous individuals. Space exploration has added a whole new dimension to the progress. Even private aviation has developed to such an advanced level of technical proficiency that it has become more routine and less a personal adventure. The individual flyer has been relegated to the sidelines, feeling a little lost as he watches aviation's march of progress being dominated by vastly expensive, increasingly organized team efforts.

Fortunately, thousands of aviation enthusiasts have found there *are* ways to recapture the sense of personal adventure in flying—by going back to the most basic forms of aviation. Soaring and hang gliding have blossomed into popular sports in recent years because they emphasize individual achievement and the challenge of coping with nature's elements. You don't have to be a trained astronaut, an aeronautical engineer, or a wealthy person to enjoy the fun of soaring and hang gliding. Nor do you need the superb physical conditioning of a professional athlete or the courage of a matador. What you do need is an interest in the natural forces that make a sailplane or a hang glider fly and the zest for mastering them through logic and skill. Anyone who has enjoyed sailing a boat, using his own ingenuity to take advantage of the elements, will appreciate the similarities in soaring and hang gliding.

This part of the book is about soaring—the sport of flying in an enclosed aircraft called a sailplane, or glider. Perhaps you've seen one of these smooth, streamlined, moterless planes wheeling silently in the sky like a great hawk. These graceful, non-polluting aircraft have an aesthetic appeal and an essential harmony with nature that make them very attractive in an increasingly ecology-minded world. They're fueled only by natural forces— updrafts of wind bouncing off mountain ridges, warm air rising from the earth's sun-heated surface (thermals), waves of air coming off mountainsides and bouncing upward from valley floors, and warm coastal air being pushed upward by cooler breezes coming off the sea. Sailplanes are designed to take advantage of these sources of lift, and when conditions are especially good, they can stay in the air as long or climb as high as any pilot could possibly wish. Sailplanes have stayed aloft for more than sixty hours, climbed to nearly 50,000 feet and traveled more than seven hundred miles on cross-country flights.

Soaring offers an exhilarating sense of freedom and achievement.

Aesthetics are certainly one of the appeals of soaring. Anyone who has flown a sailplane over New Hampshire's White Mountains on a bright fall day, as I have, has seen the brilliance of autumn foliage in a way that makes earthbound observations seem pallid. The panorama of color is viewed from a silent, floating world where only the faint rushing of wind intrudes. There is an exhilarating sense of personal freedom: freedom to explore where you never could before; freedom from the restrictions of an earthbound existence; freedom to be master of nature's forces in the sky. A soaring flight brings a sense of personal achievement that may be equaled only by other activities pitting man's skill against the elements, such as sailing. But even sailing doesn't offer the thrilling sensation of escaping the earth's confines.

"Okay," you may say, "but in a sailboat I can enjoy the challenge of mastering the elements without worrying about falling to earth from a great height." Right, but the sailplane pilot doesn't have to worry much about it either. He knows it is all but impossible for his aircraft to "fall from the sky" unless he does something *extremely* wrong. Sailing, skiing, skin diving, swimming, motorcycling, and other sports also present risks of injury and death, and soaring is as safe as these activities.

The number of deaths in soaring is very low each year, and statistics show it is safer than driving a car. In fact, the Federal Aviation Agency, which regulates soaring, allows fourteen-year-olds to fly sailplanes solo—two years before they can get automobile drivers' licenses in most states. Soaring students receive rigorous training from licensed instructors before they may fly alone, and this has helped maintain the sport's good safety record.

Sailplanes may be light, but they're built to be stronger than most light powered planes. And there's no fuel aboard to ignite in a crash landing—a major danger in power planes.

Soaring is one sport where women can compete with all men, regardless of size and strength, on an equal basis. Skill, strategy, sensitivity, and body coordination are the important factors. The number of women sailplane pilots is increasing every year, for the joy of soaring isn't limited to the strong and the athletic. If you can coordinate your mind, eyes, hands, and feet well enough to be a good automobile driver, you can be a sailplane pilot.

What is the difference between soaring and gliding? The terms are used interchangeably, even by some people involved in the sport, and you often hear the term "glider pilots." Yet there is a technical difference between gliding and soaring. Man's earliest attempts at flight usually involved gliding through the air, starting at a high point such as a hill or cliff or tower. The objective was to see how far the glider contraption would travel laterally before gravity pulled it to a landing. Pioneers, such as Otto Lilienthal, the great German glider designer, studied aerodynamics and found ways to make their craft fly steadier and farther. The Wright brothers advanced the art more by figuring the best shapes of wings to create lift from the air. Their later invention of powered flight made most people forget about gliding, but the Germans continued to perfect the art of powerless flight in the 1920s and 1930s. Their gliders stayed aloft for longer and longer periods of time, but *always gliding downward through the air to an eventual landing.* They didn't gain altitude during flight, but lost it slowly and steadily as gravity pulled them back to earth.

Soaring occurs when an aircraft *gains* altitude during flight by taking sufficient advantage of natural lift. The plane is still influenced by gravity, which provides the forward speed (its nose is pointed slightly down). This, in turn, enable the wings to produce lift. The rising air is climbing faster than the sailplane is sinking, so the plane gains altitude.

When you see a hawk or gull floating effortlessly, high overhead, its wings motionless, you are watching the soaring process. The bird has found a source of lift—probably a thermal (a column of rising warm air) or perhaps wind deflected upward off a mountain ridge. During the 1920s, increasing numbers of glider pilots found they could do the same thing. The real breakthrough for soaring came in 1929 when two German aviators named Lippisch and Kronfeld invented the variometer, an instrument that tells a pilot immediately when his aircraft is climbing or sinking. (It's difficult to judge this as quickly without the instrument when you're flying high in the air.) Now pilots could locate thermals by watching their variometers and maneuvering to stay in the rising air columns. Thus soaring was born.

The term *glider* doesn't really reflect the capabilities of today's powerless planes, since they all can soar, or gain altitude, when lift conditions are present. *Sailplane* is the preferred term for these aircraft, but many people still call them gliders. And, of course, they do glide sometimes as well as soar. In fact, the Federal Aviation Agency refers to them as gliders in its license certificates.

A license is required for soaring, just as it is for driving a car. The FAA grants the licenses, which are pilot certificates with the rating of glider pilot. It also designs and administers the tests. These are the types of ratings (or licenses) and the basic requirements:

Student license—The minimum age is fourteen, although a student may take ground instruction before he reaches that age. There is no upper age limit. The student must have completed dual flight instruction, which includes stall recovery, and must pass a written test. No physical examination is required for glider licenses, but the applicant must certify that he or she has no known physical defects that would interfere with piloting a sailplane. There is no cost for this license, which is good for two years and is renewable. The license enables a student to fly solo anytime he wishes, but he may not carry passengers.

Private license—The minimum age is sixteen, and the applicant must pass a written test as well as a flight test with an FAA examiner. The student generally studies for the written test on his own, and the FAA will furnish a list of study materials for it. He must have completed a minimum of thirty flights and ten hours of flight time. After he passes the written test and his instructor feels he's ready, the student may request the FAA flight test. He receives his license after passing the flight test. A pilot with a private license may carry passengers in his sailplane, but may not charge fees.

Commercial license—Minimum age is eighteen, and the applicant must pass a written test. He must have twenty-five hours of flight time and have completed at least one hundred flights. There is an FAA flight test for this license. Commercial glider pilots may carry passengers and may fly for hire.

Flight instructor certificate—This is required in order to give flight instruction in sailplanes. The applicant must hold a commercial pilot rating or the equivalent experience. He must pass both a written test and an FAA flight test with an examiner.

It doesn't take long to obtain a license for soaring, but naturally it depends on the individual. It's possible for a person with no experience to take a concentrated course at a soaring school on a two- or three-week vacation and qualify for his or her license to solo. From then on, the student pilot is free to go to any qualified soaring center and rent a sailplane to take up and fly alone.

If you're interested in exploring the sport of soaring, you may find it takes a bit more digging for information than some other sports. There is soaring activity in virtually every state in the country, and it is very popular in Canada, Europe, Australia, and other parts of the world. But in the United States, soaring is not the big business enterprise that powered-plane aviation is. Most soaring centers are small airports, away from the hustle and bustle of conventional airports. Many of the instructors and most of the private pilots earn their living at other jobs and devote only spare time to their first love, soaring. Others work at it full time, but chances are you might have trouble finding the nearest soaring center in the telephone directory.

The best source of information about soaring is undoubtedly the Soaring Society of America, the official organization for the sport in this country. The SSA was formed in 1932 as a non-profit organization, and the only ax it has to grind is the promotion of the sport of soaring. It is an especially efficient and helpful organization, and its staff members really care about helping you get started in soaring. They have put together an information kit with a lot of useful information. You can obtain it by sending $1.00 to:

> *Soaring Society of America*
> P.O. Box 66071
> Los Angeles, California 90066

You should also request the list of SSA governors and clubs for your region of the country. It will show you where to go and who to contact to find out about taking up soaring. The SSA can also tell you the soaring centers and schools in your region. You can become a member of the SSA by paying annual dues of $15. Members receive a subscription to *Soaring*, the organization's monthly magazine, at no extra charge. This magazine is worth the annual dues alone. It's the bible of the sport and the easiest way to keep up with what's going on. The SSA also publishes a wealth of other information and is the best single source of books, films, and other literature on soaring.

The SSA carries on a continuing national safety program as well as research and development programs. It assists local soaring groups in organizing, sanctions regional contests, administers the national championship competition, and sponsors the American teams that compete in international meets.

Once you know where the nearest gliderport is, the first thing you should do is visit it and find out if soaring really appeals to you. If it doesn't, it's better to find out now,

An introductory flight in a sailplane will let you sample soaring's appeal.

before you spend the money for lessons. You can get a fair idea by watching the sailplanes in action, talking with the pilots, and last but not least, taking an introductory flight in a two-seat trainer ship. These introductory flights are offered by almost all soaring centers, especially the ones with schools. In some vacation areas the flights are an important part of the operation. Thousands of tourists are taken on scenic flights each year at the busier centers.

The flight will probably last about half an hour, and it will cost about $10, including the tow aloft. The most common method of launching sailplanes in this country is by towing them to a good altitude with a small powered plane. The tow plane takes off, pulling the sailplane with a long polypropylene rope. The sailplane pilot simply follows the tow plane into the sky, and at about 2,000 feet he pulls a knob which releases the rope from his aircraft. Then he's free to soar, and the tow plane lands to launch the next sailplane.

There are two other methods of launching sailplanes, but neither is used very much in the United States. One is performed with a winch, which reels in a steel cable at about 50 miles an hour with the sailplane attached. This enables the plane to reach about 1,000 feet altitude before releasing.

The other is done with an automobile towing the sailplane on a steel cable until it reaches a height of about 1,300 feet.

Your flight will probably be in a Schweizer 2–33, the most commonly used trainer sailplane in the United States. It has dual controls, which means that you will have a set of controls exactly like those the pilot uses. The pilot sits in the rear seat, leaving the passenger in front with a spectacular view through the bubble canopy. It's an exhilarating way to be introduced to soaring.

Your pilot will be a highly experienced one, since he must hold a commercial pilot rating to fly paying passengers. Like all soaring pilots, he's in love with the sport, and his enthusiasm is apt to be contagious. He'll probably be eager to answer your questions and explain how the sailplane works. And he'll allow you to take over the controls and try a series of turns and maneuvers once you're aloft. You'll be surprised at the responsiveness of the sailplane as you use the controls and the perfect sense of ability to make the ship go anywhere you want it to. You'll marvel at the stillness and the feeling of floating like a bird—a bird completely in control in the sky.

When it's time to land, the pilot will bring the sailplane over the field in a prescribed landing pattern and push the control stick forward to make the ship descend at the desired rate. You'll come in over the runway and land at a slower speed than powered planes do—45-50 miles per hour is the average for many sailplanes. The landing will probably be so soft and easy that you'll scarcely notice the point at which you're rolling along on the ground. In a minute you'll be unsnapping your shoulder harness and climbing out of the sailplane, regretting that the flight is over.

Take a look around the gliderport while you're there and you'll see that soaring is a very informal, outdoor sport. No one dresses in elaborately fashionable sports clothing. Sweatshirts, T-shirts, jeans, sweaters, and wind-breakers are most commonly seen, depending on the weather. You can easily engage strangers in conversation about soaring because devotees of this sport love to talk about it. Luxurious buildings and lounges are practically unheard of at soaring sites, so be prepared to rough it. You may have to warm up in your car if it's a cold day or seek a shady spot on some grass if it's a hot one. The one consistent quality you'll notice is a cheerfulness on the part of everyone—even the friends and relatives of pilots, who often bring picnic lunches and enjoy the outdoors.

If the soaring center you visit has a school, don't hesitate to ask plenty of questions about the length of time it takes to complete the course, the methods of teaching and the costs. Most schools have brochures containing much of this information, but ask for more if it needs explaining. You should inquire about package plans that offer instruction from beginner level to a license. And ask if the instructor's time and the tow-plane fee are included in the rates quoted. If the total cost seems too much for you at that time, discuss it with the school director. He might well work out some arrangement for time payment so you can start lessons right away, rather than wait until you have saved enough for a complete course.

Soaring is not the least expensive sport in the world, but its costs compare favorably with those of skiing, golf, and sailing. It will generally cost about $500 at a soaring school to become a proficient pilot with a private license. It would be less, of course, to reach the student-license level where you are allowed to fly alone for your own enjoyment. Skiing lessons, equipment, and lodging often cost more than this, and instruction by a golf or tennis pro is usually more than $10 per hour. The average cost of renting a sailplane and being towed aloft is about $15 an hour —but the fun of being around a gliderport, talking shop, picnicking, and generally having a good time is free! It's easy to make an afternoon of it.

One popular way to cut costs is to join one of the more than 180 soaring clubs in the United States. These clubs own their own planes, which members can fly free. Some of them offer free instruction, and others charge modest fees. There is usually an initiation fee of one to two hundred dollars, which buys your share of the club's sailplanes, and modest monthly dues. The Soaring Society of America has a complete directory of clubs and can put you in touch with those nearest you. You'll want to consider carefully before joining a club, to be sure it offers what you want in soaring. Some clubs are more formal than others, but all require that members cooperate and help around the field. The camaraderie of fellow soaring enthusiasts is an important benefit, and clubs often become social organizations as well as flying units. By choosing one with people you think you'll enjoy, you can make your soaring even more fun.

If you really get into the sport of soaring, you'll probably reach a point when you'll wonder whether you should rent sailplanes or purchase one. Cost will be the big factor, plus your level of soaring activity. If your principal enjoyment is going to a nearby gliderport for an afternoon of fun in local flying, you'd be better off to rent sailplanes as you need them. (In a club you may not even have to do that.) If you become an avid soaring pilot who flies frequent cross-country trips and enters local, regional, and national competition meets, you'll probably want to have your own aircraft.

It's a pretty heavy investment—but that's just what it is, an investment. You stand an excellent chance of getting most of your money back if you decide to sell, because sailplanes depreciate very little in value, due to strong demand for used craft. Sailplanes don't wear out fast—there's no complex engine and fuel system requiring overhauling. New American-made models start at about $5,000, and you can pay up to $20,000 for the fanciest, high-performance European aircraft. Buying a factory kit with plans and assembling the sailplane yourself can cut the cost in half. But assembling the sailplane is no simple task. It will probably take all your spare time for about six months, and it will require a suitably large and sheltered space in which to work. (Sailplanes, of course, are designed so that the wings can be quickly disassembled from the fuselage for transportation on a trailer.) An FAA inspector is legally required to examine your assembly work at several points before the sailplane can be certified for flight. This is one of the many safeguards that have helped make soaring a safe sport.

You can choose from many types of sailplanes, but the beginner would do well to consider the several time-proven, reliable models most widely used in the United States. Schweizer Aircraft Corporation of Elmira, New

The most popular sailplane in America is Schweizer's model 1–26.

York, the only major American manufacturer, makes most of them, although there are several very good models made by much smaller manufacturers. The most popular sailplane in America is Schweizer's model 1–26. More than five hundred of these are in use, and about two hundred of them were sold as kits and built by the owners. The 1–26 is a neat little all-metal single-seater, used for personal fun flying as well as for competition in meets. The basic design hasn't been changed since its introduction many years ago. Modifications over the years have been calculated not to change its flight characteristics. This was planned so there would be a one-design class of sailplanes which would enable pilots to compete in meets with equal equipment. Many soaring enthusiasts believe this is the only fair way to judge pilots' flying ability. There is an active 1–26 association, whose members get together in meets regularly. The 1–26 is regarded by just about everybody as fast, safe, and fun.

If you take flying lessons, you'll probably learn in Schweizer's model 2–33, the most widely used trainer sailplane in this country. It's a 2-place, high-wing, all-metal aircraft and is considered extremely rugged and easy to fly. It soars well in even light lift conditions, and it is often used to take passengers for introductory rides. The 2–33 is also popular with soaring clubs.

A model frequently used for advanced instruction is Schweizer's 2–32. This all-metal 2-seat sailplane is more luxuriously appointed inside than the 2–33, and its mid-wing construction offers excellent visibility. It's popular with soaring clubs and with pilots who want to take relatives and friends on flights. The back seat can accommodate two passengers and the pilot sits in front. It's a very versatile aircraft and its performance is rated as the best in the world for multi-place sailplanes.

Beyond this, there are the high-performance sailplanes, mostly fiber-glass models made in Europe. These light, streamlined craft have extra-long, thin wings designed to provide the maximum in lift. They're used in competition and they're very expensive. A sailplane's performance ability is expressed in terms of its *glide ratio,* or lift-to-drag (L/D) ratio. This is the aircraft's best angle of glide, or the maximum distance it can travel laterally for every foot of altitude it loses in still air. Thus, a sailplane with a 25-to-1 L/D ratio will travel 25 feet forward for every foot that it loses in altitude. This, incidentally, is the ratio of 2-place sailplanes. Any model with a glide ratio of 30-to-1 or above is considered high-performance. The best competition sailplanes have ratios ranging nearly as high as 50-to-1.

A new American high-performance craft is the Schweizer model 1–35.

The glide ratio of the average sailplane is about three times better than that of light powered planes. For example, the Piper Cub J3C-65, a very light, single-engine plane, has a glide ratio of 10-to-1.

Schweizer recently introduced a new, high-performance model called the 1–35, designed to compete with the best European aircraft. Schweizer decided to construct it of metal instead of fiber glass, but it is even lighter than most of the fiber-glass models. The 1–35 is expected to take a prominent place among the high performance sailplanes.

The range of sailplane models is very wide, but the

majority of soaring enthusiasts find all the fun they need without flying the expensive, high-performance models. The range of people who enjoy soaring is just as wide as that of the planes available. Many doctors, lawyers, businessmen, and airline pilots are enthusiastic participants in this sport, but so are many high school students, college students, truck drivers, and clerical workers. You can choose a level of participation and cost to suit yourself.

2

What Makes Sailplanes Soar?

You may have heard someone say about sailplanes, "You wouldn't get me up in one of those things without a motor for a million dollars." People who say this are afraid, of course. They're afraid that an aircraft without the power of an engine will fall to earth and crash. Fear is often based on the unknown, and in this case it stems from lack of understanding of the principles of flight. They don't know that there are natural forces keeping the plane aloft.

When a person takes up soaring, among the first things he or she is taught at a flight school are the basic principles of aerodynamics. The reasoning is that if a student understands what laws of physics keep a sailplane in the air and what brings it back to earth, he will be dealing with known facts, not scary mysteries. He'll realize that these facts have been proved millions of times, and that they're immutable laws of science. And he won't be wondering, "Are we going to fall to earth?" when he takes his flight lessons.

The science of aerodynamics has been greatly refined

over the years, with many theories, rules, and formulas adding to the basic knowledge. But it isn't necessary for a soaring pilot to understand more than a couple of basic principles. One of these is Bernoulli's principle, the most basic in all of aviation. It states that the pressure of a liquid or gas decreases where the speed of either one increases. To understand how this applies to airplanes, take a look at the wing of any aircraft. It's not flat, with uniform thickness, like a board. The front, or leading edge, is thicker than the rear, or trailing edge, and it is curved. While the underside of the wing is relatively flat, the top side is curved. Engineers have designed it that way so that it forms what is called an air foil. When an aircraft is moving in flight, air is forced past the wing. The flow of air is split by the leading edge; some goes over the top and some under the wing, then it meets at the trailing edge. The air traveling over the curved top must go a greater distance than that traveling along the flat bottom surface. So it goes faster to catch up with the air underneath, and this reduces the pressure on top of the wing. Since the pressure beneath the wing is greater, it forces the wing upward, and this is called *lift*.

Lift is created beneath an airplane wing when the air pressure is greater than that above the wing. Air going over the top travels faster and farther, which decreases pressure.

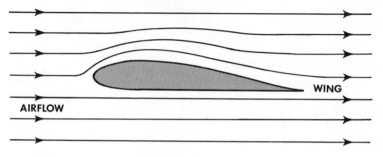

BERNOUILLI'S LAW

This is a constant law. Different means are employed to force sufficient air past the wing, but the result is the same. All that is needed is *thrust* to move the aircraft forward, so the wing will cut into the air. A propeller pulls the plane forward by "biting" into the air; a jet engine pushes the plane forward by discharging exhaust gases. A sailplane depends on the pull of gravity to move it forward at a slight downward angle. If the thrust provides sufficient forward motion, the wings cannot help but produce lift.

A sailplane doesn't fly fast enough to produce lift that is greater than the force of gravity making the plane descend, so it is always going down—except when it is in rising air, such as a thermal. But it only goes down gradually since there is always some lift being produced in normal flight to counteract gravity. Thus, there is no way that a sailplane can simply fall straight down unless the pilot steers it straight down or maneuvers it in such a way that

Forward motion produces lift under a sailplane's wings, but drag, created by turbulence, and gravity are forces that work in opposition to lift.

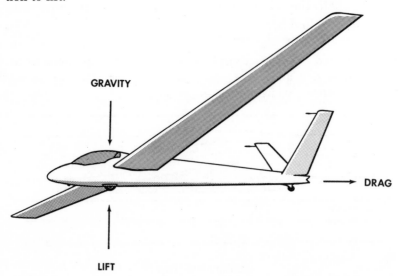

GRAVITY

DRAG

LIFT

the wings no longer produce lift. When this occurs, it is called a *stall*, and that brings us to another aerodynamic principle: *the angle of attack.*

The angle of attack is simply the angle at which the wing meets the air, or "attacks" it in flight. The shapes of wings are designed to accommodate Bernoulli's principle, with air sliding smoothly over and under the wing at different speeds and producing lift. But if you pull back on the control stick and point the nose of a sailplane too far upwards, a peculiar thing happens. The angle at which the wing meets the air (the angle of attack) becomes so sharp that the flowing air cannot curve enough to follow the top surface of the wing. Instead, it tumbles and becomes turbulence at the rear of the wing. Turbulence produces a force called *drag*, which works in opposition to lift. When drag overpowers the lift being produced by the wing, the wing is said to be stalled. It is no longer producing lift, and the plane is no longer flying. Now there are no forces to prevent it from falling to earth like any other object.

In practice, however, this situation isn't as deadly as it sounds, providing the sailplane is cruising at a sufficiently high altitude to allow time to recover from the stall. Sailplanes are designed so that the nose is heavier than the tail —in other words, the center of gravity is toward the front of the plane. When the wing stalls and the ship starts to fall, the nose quickly comes down lower than the tail. This brings the plane's position back to a more favorable angle of attack and increases the speed. Bernoulli's principle starts working again, lift is created, and the sailplane is gliding again. Many sailplanes will actually recover from stalls by themselves in this manner, but the pilot should effect the recovery himself by pointing the nose down, keeping the wings level and then leveling off. Students receive extensive stall-recovery practice in their earliest

flying lessons. The time when a stall can be really dangerous is when the sailplane is at a low altitude, such as on a
landing approach, and there isn't time to recover. If a pilot
follows normal flying procedures, he will never find himself in that situation.

Another cause of stalls is allowing the aircraft to slow
down so much that there isn't sufficient velocity in the air
flowing over and under the wing to produce lift. Pilots
avoid this by simply keeping an eye on the airspeed indicator and pushing the control stick forward to increase airspeed to a level above that at which stalling can occur.
Manufacturers state the stalling speeds of all aircraft, and
all pilots should know them. Recovery is made with the
same procedure we just described.

We've discussed the aerodynamic principles of forces
that enable a sailplane to glide, and we know what keeps it
from plummeting to earth. But what about the forces that
enable it to *climb* and soar? To understand these it will be
necessary to learn something about meteorology, and if
you take up soaring, you'll find yourself increasingly interested in the behavior of winds, thermals, and clouds. You'll
study basic meteorology in any soaring school, and the
more you get into it, the more complex and fascinating it
will become. In a short time you'll have a good working
knowledge of weather and its effect on soaring.

Briefly, there are four main types of natural lift for
sailplanes to exploit. The first is *ridge* lift, which was dis-
covered by early glider pilots before any of the other
forms. It is produced when prevailing winds encounter
vertical obstacles such as hills or ridges. The wind strikes
the hill or ridge and is deflected upward and over it in a
sort of wave formation. Steady winds blowing against the
side of a ridge provide ideal soaring conditions, and a
sailplane flying in these upward-bouncing winds can often

stay aloft all day if the pilot wishes. It is an especially good form of lift for a beginning pilot because it is the easiest type of updraft in which to fly. There's less chance of losing the lift, and you can often stay up for longer periods than with the other types. If the gliderport where you take lessons has a nearby ridge with good prevailing winds, you'll have excellent learning conditions.

Your instructor will show you how to cruise back and forth along the length of the ridge, taking advantage of this steady lift. He'll explain the basic precautions of all ridge flying. You won't fly over the crest of the ridge, because you could get caught in the wind as it goes over the top and descends on the other side, where there are downdrafts and turbulence. Instead, you'll soar above the side of the ridge where the wind is striking, and you'll stay a respectable distance away from ridge surface itself, to avoid being blown into the trees. You'll make all your turns *away* from the ridge when you turn around to retrace your flight path along the length of it. This puts you out over lower land and gives you room to descend if you lose the lift while turning.

The lift along a ridge varies in spots, depending on the shape of the obstructing slope and the direction and speed of the wind. Some parts of the ridge are higher than others; some have wooded slopes and others smooth; some slopes are like cliffs and others gentle. All these conditions affect the lift in any given spot. In flying back and forth along the ridge you'll do well to note the strongest lift locations on your variometer and return to them to gain altitude. In the areas of zero or negative lift it's best to push the stick forward, increase your airspeed and leave them as soon as possible to avoid losing altitude. After all, you're flying up there to stay aloft and have fun; you don't want to have to give up and fly back to the field early. Ridge soaring makes you want to keep flying as long as possible.

Another favorite form of lift for soaring buffs is *thermals*. These columns of rising warm air offer different benefits from those of ridge lift. They don't have the steady longevity of ridge lift; you ride one to the top and then fly off to seek another. But they can often lift you higher than ridge conditions, and there is the challenge of finding them when they can't be seen.

Thermals can be found everywhere in the world—in hot climates or in cold winter climates. They are caused by the different rates at which the sun heats the earth. The earth, in turn, heats the air in some places more intensely than it does in others. When we speak of warm air we are speaking only in relative terms; it is warmer than the air surrounding it, and thus lighter. For instance, the air above a large paved area receives reflected heat and rises. A soaring pilot in search of thermals will look for areas that are likely to reflect the sun's heat, such as plowed fields, beaches, and hillsides with no trees. They avoid green fields and woods since they absorb solar heat. Thermals can be found, of course, only on days when the sky isn't overcast.

The challenge of finding thermals is made trickier by the fact that since you can't see them you never know until you fly into one whether it is narrow, wide, or relatively tall. There are a few signs to watch for. A puffy cumulus cloud is usually the cap on a thermal. Warm, moist air has risen to a height where it has cooled enough for the moisture to condense and form the cloud.

When thermal-seeking pilots spot such a cloud they fly under it to exploit the rising air. Thermals can lift a sailplane very quickly: usually 300 to 400 feet per minute up to about 8,000 feet. Pilots should always avoid riding the thermal up into a cumulus cloud, however. Such clouds

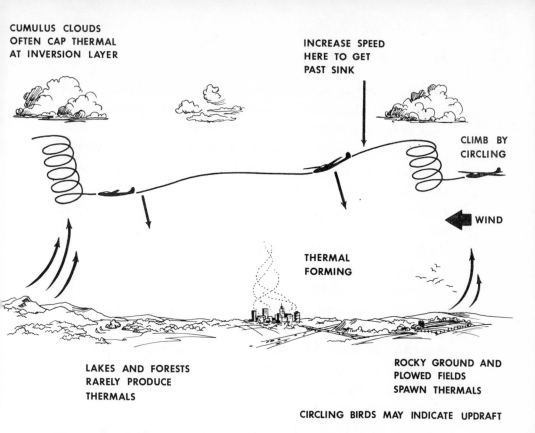

CUMULUS CLOUDS
OFTEN CAP THERMAL
AT INVERSION LAYER

INCREASE SPEED
HERE TO GET
PAST SINK

CLIMB BY
CIRCLING

WIND

THERMAL
FORMING

LAKES AND FORESTS
RARELY PRODUCE
THERMALS

ROCKY GROUND AND
PLOWED FIELDS
SPAWN THERMALS

CIRCLING BIRDS MAY INDICATE UPDRAFT

The soaring pilot is constantly searching for thermals to gain altitude.

often contain dangerous turbulence, and it's illegal to fly into them in the United States.

Another sign to watch for is a circling hawk or buzzard. These feathered friends are experts at soaring and at finding thermals. Following them is usually a good bet if they're circling. Of course, birds can fly tighter circles than can sailplanes, and they might be in a narrow thermal which a plane can't exploit.

The way to ride a thermal is to circle tightly in order to stay within its confines. Without a variometer it would be very difficult to know when you're in the center of a thermal or when you're on the outer edge where the lift is weaker. Even with a variometer, it takes some calculating. You're never sure when you first notice some lift whether you're coming upon a strong thermal or the end of one that is expiring. There are as many methods of locating thermals as there are pilots.

One method is to count off the seconds that elapse from the time your variometer begins rising until it starts showing decline. You keep flying straight through the lift, then turn, come around and fly through it again at 90° to your original course. Now you know where the strongest lift is, and you quickly fly back into it and circle tightly.

Another method is to turn immediately when your variometer shows lift and start circling to take advantage of it. Of course, you may be in a weaker part of the thermal rather than the center, but you'll be getting some lift. Then you can gradually broaden your turns to explore the surrounding area and see if the lift is stronger nearby. The mysteries of thermal lift present a never-ending game, and it's part of the fun of soaring.

The third type of lift is not found in as many locations as the first two, but it's the most dramatic of all. It's called *mountain wave,* or lee wave, or just wave soaring. It has carried sailplanes to altitudes far beyond those provided by the other forms of lift: nearly 50,000 feet. When conditions are right, a stream of fast-moving air will strike a mountain and pass over it and down the other side. Then it will bounce upward to great heights in the form of a giant wave. It is similar to the action of water in a river passing swiftly over a submerged rock and forming waves behind it. Pilots have learned that the waves appearing near the lee side of the mountain can offer incredibly good soaring. It is usually very smooth. There are two types of clouds that are sometimes signs of mountain waves: a cap cloud, which sits atop the mountain, and a lenticular-shaped cloud at a high altitude off the lee side of the mountain.

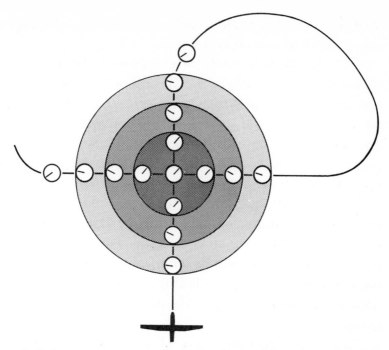

To find the center of a thermal, the pilot watches his variometer readings, finds the highest rate of lift, then turns and crosses this point at 90°.

THE LEE WAVE

Lee waves, or mountain waves, bounce to great heights and can provide the most dramatic soaring conditions of all.

Spotting these is enough to send many a soaring pilot up in eager search of mountain-wave lift.

The fourth type of lift for sailplanes is the *sea breeze*. This is a condition where the air on land becomes heated and begins to rise at a time when cooler sea air is coming off the water as wind. It rushes in like a wedge under the warmer air and forces it upward. Cumulus clouds frequently form as the rising warm air releases its moisture. It's usually a fairly narrow band of lift since sea breezes seldom penetrate more than a few miles inland. It's possible to fly along it much as you would fly along a ridge, and you'll know when you stray over the boundary of it because suddenly there will be no lift at all. But while you're soaring in it, you're apt to find it can provide a very substantial amount of lift and make an enjoyable afternoon of flying.

These are nature's ways of keeping those graceful sailplanes silently aloft. Natures provides free, non-polluting energy, and it's nearly as efficient as most other fuels.

3

Flying the Sailplane

We know the natural forces that enable a sailplane to glide and to soar. We know that the wings are designed to take advantage of Bernoulli's principle and create lift when there is forward motion of the aircraft. Now let's take a look at the controls that enable a pilot to maneuver a sailplane in the air.

For the most part, a sailplane is built like any other airplane without its engines. The basic parts are similar: wings, fuselage, fin, rudder, elevators, horizontal stabilizer, and ailerons. The wings and the parts of the tail assembly are the sections of the aircraft directly affected by aerodynamic forces. The movable parts of them are called control surfaces.

Aircraft movement is controlled as it acts on three axes: the longitudinal or *roll* axis, the lateral or *pitch* axis, and the vertical or *yaw* axis (see diagram). These axes are perpendicular to each other and pass through the plane's center of gravity.

The longitudinal axis is best described as an imaginary line running from the nose to the tail. Motion about this axis is called *roll*. It is controlled by the ailerons—hinged sections of the wing on the trailing edge, out near

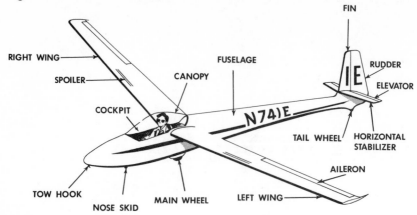

The basic parts of a sailplane.

the wing tip. They're connected so that when the pilot makes one of them deflect up, the other deflects down. The aileron which is deflected down causes more lift on that wing, while the one that is deflected up interferes with the flow of air over the top of that wing and reduces lift. This generates a downward force. This makes the aircraft roll or bank toward the up aileron as the opposite wing lifts.

The lateral axis runs from one wing tip to the other, and the plane changes *pitch* when it rotates on this axis. The elevator controls this motion. This is the back part of the horizontal stabilizer, which moves on a hinge. The name isn't entirely accurate since the elevator not only causes the plane to go up, but to go down as well. When it is deflected upward it causes the air to strike the top surface, which provides a downward force on the tail. With the tail being pushed down, the airplane rotates about its lateral axis, and the nose goes up. When the elevator is deflected downward, the opposite occurs: air pushes the tail up, and the nose goes down.

The vertical axis is an imaginary line running through the aircraft like a spindle, from top to bottom. When the

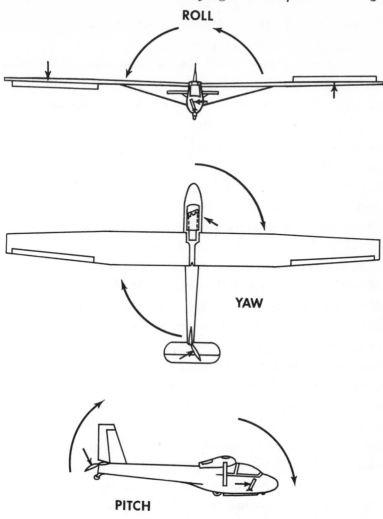

Aircraft movement is controlled as it acts on three axes: longi-tudinal (roll), vertical (yaw) and lateral (pitch).

plane moves about this axis it is called *yaw*. This motion is controlled by the rudder, which is the hinged part connected to the rear of the fin. When the rudder is moved to the right, the air strikes its right side, causing a force that pushes the tail to the left. This makes the plane rotate on its vertical axis, or yaw, moving the nose to the right. Move the rudder to the left and the opposite happens: the force yaws the plane's nose to the left.

Another control you'll see on sailplanes is called a *spoiler*. This is a flat surface that may be raised out of the top side of each wing. It disrupts the air flow over the wing, destroying lift and also producing drag. *Air brakes* act in a similar manner, extending downward from the bottom of the wing and adding more drag. A pilot uses spoilers and air brakes to slow the sailplane down and to descend more quickly. This is often useful when he is approaching the field for a landing.

How does a pilot move the various control surfaces when he wants to maneuver the sailplane? They are connected by cables, torque tubes, and push-pull rods to the pilot's controls in the cockpit. He uses pedals, like the clutch and brake pedals in a car, to control the rudder. He uses a control stick, extending out of the floor between his knees, to control the ailerons and the elevator. When he pushes on the right pedal, it moves the rudder to the right and the plane's nose yaws to the right. If he moves the stick to the right, the left aileron deflects downward, the right aileron moves upward, and the sailplane rolls or banks to the right. If he pulls the stick back, the elevator deflects up and the plane rotates nose up on the lateral axis. When he pushes the stick forward, the elevator deflects down, the tail is pushed up and the nose goes down. When he wants to move the spoilers he uses a separate handle.

When you learn to drive a car, you learn to coordinate the movements of your hands and feet on the controls to make the car do what you want it to. The same is true in piloting a sailplane. In your early lessons, your instructor will stress practice in coordinating control movements. You'll learn to turn the sailplane by using the rudder and ailerons in the right combination to prevent the plane from slipping or skidding sideways. And you'll learn not to pull the stick back too fast or too far, because this may increase the angle of attack to the point where the wing will stall.

Coordinating the controls will soon become second nature to you. Using the controls correctly, you'll be able to turn, dive, and make the sailplane climb, increase and decrease your speed, and generally move your aircraft around in the air with a great deal of precision.

One of the appeals of soaring is that it's a sport where you learn by doing, almost from the start. A soaring school will give you plenty of study in theory, techniques, and safety, of course. Chances are, your textbook will be Carle Conway's excellent book, *The Joy of Soaring*, which is the Soaring Society of America's official instruction manual. And you'll want to study Richard A. Wolters' handsome *The Art and Technique of Soaring*, the most impressive book yet written on the subject. But from your very first lesson, you'll be handling the controls—*flying* the sailplane. And before long, you'll be doing 90 per cent of the flying in each lesson, having the fun of soaring while you learn.

Your flight lessons will follow a planned order, and the instructor will make sure you have learned one lesson before moving on to the next. He keeps a record of training for each student, to show what each flight lesson covered and the student's ability achieved during that lesson. You will also keep a log of your flying time and the type of lesson covered in each flight, for your own use. The instructor usually fills it in for you and signs it after each flight.

Despite the camaraderie and feeling of cheerfulness around a gliderport, one thing is taken very seriously, and that is safety. Instructors, weekend pilots, and people helping out around the field have one thing in common besides their love for soaring, and that is their no-nonsense attitude about safety. Rules and procedures are strictly observed by everyone. If parents or spouses have any doubt about the safety of anyone taking up this sport, they should spend some time around a gliderport and observe the prevailing attitude. There are rigid rules about where you can park your car, where you may walk and how close you may get to an aircraft. These are necessary to prevent visitors from wandering into the path of planes landing or taking off, and to prevent accidental damage to the vital control surfaces of sailplanes on the ground.

The instructor will brief you before the flight on the maneuvers to be practiced. Then he'll lead you out to the sailplane to make the preflight inspection *required before every flight,* regardless of the number of times the plane has already flown that day. He'll show you how to examine every item on the standard inspection list, then he'll let you make the inspection while he looks on. You'll soon get into the reflex habit of checking every bolt and connector that holds the wing, fuselage, tail assembly, and other parts of the sailplane together. You'll check the control actuating rods and connecting rods to be sure they're connected properly and that they make the control surfaces work. You'll also inspect the entire external surface for cracks, tears, or dents. Such a close inspection may seem unnecessary, but a pilot should never assume that "someone else has checked it, so it must be okay." Finding out at 3,000 or 4,000 feet in the air that "someone else" made a mistake could be a very unpleasant experience.

You'll start to become familiar with the instrument panel from the time you first take your place in the front seat of the cockpit. The number of instruments you'll see will vary, depending on the sailplane. Some of them aren't necessary in training flights. A compass is useful in cross-country flights, but not for local flying. Instruments like turn-and-bank indicators aren't used in local soaring. The three basic instruments you'll need are the airspeed indicator, the variometer, and the altimeter.

You will soon learn that the airspeed indicator is very important in soaring. You'll need it to make sure you stay above your sailplane's stalling speed, to maintain the best glide angle, and to help you make landing approaches at the safest speeds. Airspeed isn't necessarily the same as ground speed; this instrument tells you how fast your sailplane is moving through the air. Your airspeed may be 75 miles per hour, but you'll only travel 50 miles in an hour over the ground if there is a headwind of 25 miles per hour blowing at you.

The variometer tells a pilot the rate at which he is gaining or losing altitude, and it's the instrument watched most closely when looking for thermals or other types of lift. It responds more quickly than the altimeter to indicate when a sailplane enters an area of lift. There are two types: dial face and pellet. The dial-face type indicates with a needle how many feet per minute you're losing or gaining altitude. The pellet type employs two tubes with red and green balls in them. It's activated by change in atmospheric pressure as the sailplane climbs or descends. When the green balls rise in their tube, the aircraft is rising. When the red balls rise, the plane is losing altitude. It's a very simple and reliable instrument.

The altimeter simply tells how many feet a sailplane is above sea level. Or it can be set to show how many feet the plane is above ground level in a particular place. It works according to changes in air pressure—the higher you go, the less air pressure. This causes the needle on the altimeter to show a higher altitude. Since the weather on any given day causes changes in atmospheric pressure, a pilot should always check with the airport control tower (if there is one), the flight office at the gliderport, or a local weather service for the barometric reading. Then he can set the altimeter for this reading with a knob. This will give him his correct altitude above sea level when he's in the air. He knows the elevation of the gliderport, and this is sufficient for most soaring flights.

The remainder of the preflight check takes place inside the cockpit, while you're waiting for the ground handler to bring the end of the tow line from the tow plane, 200 feet ahead of you. Many pilots try to memorize the check list in abc order:

a. Altimeter properly set.
b. Belt and shoulder harness fastened and tightened so you won't bounce and strike your head in a sudden stop or severe turbulence.
c. Canopy properly closed and secured.
c. Controls checked to be sure they are all working. This means looking out the canopy and observing rudder, elevator, and aileron movement as you activate the controls.
c. Check wind sock for direction of wind.

The final part of the preflight check is made with the help of the ground crewman who hooks your sailplane to the tow rope. The tow plane is going to pull you off the runway and up to 2,000 or maybe 3,000 feet above the field on the end of a slim but strong nylon or polypropylene rope. The tow-plane pilot can release the rope from his plane, but normal procedure is for the sailplane pilot to release it from the hook in the nose of his aircraft when he has reached the desired altitude for soaring. You want to make sure it is securely hooked on the sailplane before you take off. And you want to make sure the release mechanism will work with you're in the air and it's time to release the rope.

To check this, the ground crewman yells, "Open!" and you pull on the big red knob in front of you. This opens the circular hook so he can place the tow rope ring into it. Now he calls, "Close!" and you release the knob. He tests it by yanking on the rope, then calls for you to release it. After you pull the knob once more, he inserts the ring in the hook again and you close it. Now you're ready.

Being towed for a takeoff is not really a difficult procedure, yet most student pilots are nervous the first few times they try it. The instructor encourages you to take the controls on takeoff very early in your lessons, even though he may keep a hand lightly on the controls in case he has to make a quick correction. Your hands are usually perspiring by the time the ground crewman asks, "Ready?" and you signal yes by moving an index finger in a circle. The tow plane pilot guns his engine and moves forward until the rope slack is taken up. Now he waggles his rudder as a signal that he's ready. He waits for you to respond by pushing your rudder pedals left and right.

The tow plane starts to move down the runway, pulling the sailplane bumpily along on its single wheel. The ground crewman runs along with the sailplane, holding one wing tip up to keep it balanced until it is going fast enough for the control surfaces to work. As you roll along, gaining speed, the control stick should be kept in a neutral position, neither forward nor backward. But then it should be brought back slowly with gentle pressure to increase the angle of attack. Now the wings are starting to work, and in a moment the rumbling beneath you stops and you realize you are airborne, skimming along ever-so-slightly off the ground.

Of course, the tow plane is increasing speed steadily as it roars along the ground, preparing for takeoff. You're off before he is, and the increasing speed could cause the sailplane to shoot into the air like a kite if you held the stick back. So you apply a slight pressure forward on the stick to avoid this. Otherwise you might soar above the tow plane and pull its tail up, making it impossible for him to take off.

It isn't necessary to look at your wings to see if they're level. You can tell by looking at the tow plane and the horizon in relation to the shape of your windshield. You can level the wings by moving the control stick to the right or left slightly. As you become more advanced in your lessons, the instructor will show you how to angle the sailplane into the wind when there's a crosswind, so you'll track the same path as the tow plane.

Now the tow plane is rising rapidly into the air and you're being pulled along serenely, leaving the field far below. It should be peaceful, but most students find that flying tow is one of the hardest things to do during their early lessons. The sailplane is being pulled so fast that it easily reacts to any movement of the controls. So easily, in fact, that the student pilot finds himself over-correcting whenever he tries to maneuver the plane. If left on its own, the sailplane will tend to climb too far above the tow plane, and this usually happens before the student realizes he's getting out of position. He looks down in horror on the tow plane dropping below him and he shoves the stick forward to get back down there. It's too much of a shove, and the sailplane dives until it drops too far below the tow plane. Now the student pulls the stick back too far, and his plane shoots up too high again. Most instructors let their students struggle with this, as long as they don't get too far out of position. It takes several such experiences before most student pilots get the "feel" of being towed and realize that very small movements with the stick and rudder can keep the sailplane smoothly behind the tow plane.

Early lessons include piloting the sailplane while being towed aloft.

Once they have learned it, they usually wonder why they had so much trouble flying on tow in the first place.

The tow plane creates a "prop wash" or area of turbulence behind it, and the sailplane pilot should avoid flying in it, mainly because it's bumpy and makes it harder to control the aircraft. Two towing positions are flown to avoid this turbulence: high tow and low tow. High tow is the most commonly used. In this position, the sailplane flies in smooth air just above the prop wash. You'll become accustomed to judging when you are in the correct position for high tow by seeing the tow plane's position in your windshield. The same holds true for low-tow position, which is sometimes used if the tow plane is having trouble climbing fast enough on takeoff. As you gain experience you'll learn other fine points of the tow, such as smooth

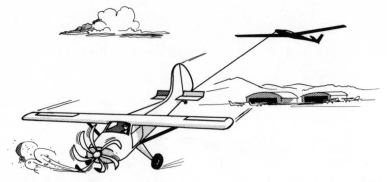

Applying forward pressure on the stick prevents the sailplane from climbing faster than the tow plane and pulls its tail up.

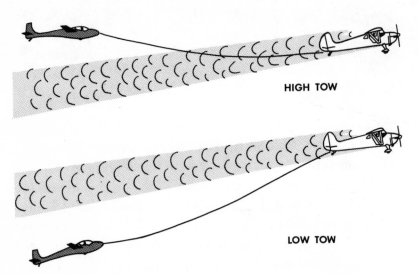

HIGH TOW

LOW TOW

These two main towing positions are used to avoid turbulence.

turns when the tow plane turns and keeping the rope from going slack.

You'll also be required to practice safety procedures to use if the tow rope should ever break. You will drill in procedures for gliding back to the field for landing over and over again, until it becomes second nature to you.

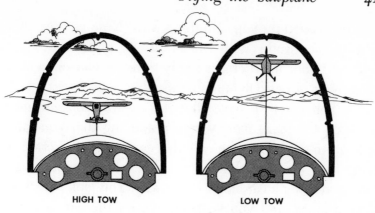

HIGH TOW   LOW TOW

TO HOLD POSITION VERTICALLY KEEP
TOWPLANE IN POSITION ON GLIDER'S WINDSHELD

Ropes seldom break, but every sailplane pilot must be prepared for that eventuality.

As you approach the altitude agreed upon for release of the sailplane, you should look around you to be sure there are no other aircraft nearby. As a student pilot, you should always release while you are upwind of the gliderport, so you can easily glide back to a landing. Now you reach for that red release knob and pull. You'll hear and feel a thump and then you'll see the rope spring free in front of you. Now you're suddenly free—high in the air, with no more power source to pull you. The first time this happens, you feel as though you have cut the umbilical cord, but later you welcome the release because you're now free to soar.

Immediately after you see the tow rope spring free, there is a standard maneuver to execute. The tow plane makes a diving left turn to get out of the area as quickly as possible. At the same time, the sailplane pilot makes a climbing turn to the right, in the opposite direction from the tow plane, to minimize any chance of collision. You're traveling well above cruising speed when you release, because you have been towed. You can use this extra speed to gain lift as you do your climbing turn. Now you are flying at a good altitude, with full ability to glide back to the field, and your instructor is ready to teach you some of the maneuvers of basic flying in a sailplane.

When you're a new pilot it's easy to concentrate so much on the maneuvers you're practicing that you fail to look around you to see whether any other aircraft are flying near you. Yet this is just as important as it is when you are driving a car along a highway. You look before you change lanes, and you keep an eye on the cars ahead of you because they could suddenly slow down or stop. You also look before making a turn off the highway onto another road. A soaring pilot must do the same thing in the air. This is called *clearing* the area, and your instructor will catch you every time you fail to do it before starting a maneuver. It requires a bit more effort in a sailplane, because visibility is blocked in some areas by parts of the sailplane. And there is no rear view mirror—that would create too much drag on the outside of the plane. So you turn your head and look in all directions, including above and below you.

There are really only two basic maneuvers used in flying a sailplane: the straight glide and the turn. Just about everything you do in controlling the sailplane stems from these. The straight glide is the easiest, of course. It simply requires keeping the wings level, the airspeed at the best level and, therefore, the angle of attack at its most efficient. You won't have any trouble mastering this basic part of flying.

Making a proper turn will require a bit more practice because more than one control is used to do it. The rudder alone doesn't make a sailplane turn, although it causes it to yaw to the left or right on its vertical axis. Nor do you use the ailerons alone to turn the plane by banking to the right or left. The down aileron would create more drag than the up aileron, and this tends to turn the plane in the opposite direction from where you intend to turn. It's called *adverse yaw*. To offset this force, you need to turn the rudder in the direction of the intended turn at the same time. So, to make a left turn, you push gently and steadily on the left rudder while simultaneously applying a little pressure to the left of the stick. This is called a *coordinated turn,* something you will hear over and over again from your instructor.

A coordinated turn will be a smooth one, with the wings pulling the sailplane through it. If the turn isn't well coordinated, you'll be able to tell at a glance by looking at the *yaw string*. This simple device consists of a piece of string or yarn attached to the plane in front of the canopy. It should be streaming straight back at you. If it is fluttering to the right when you're executing a left turn, it means you haven't applied enough left rudder to counteract the adverse yaw. You'll also need to pull back gently on the stick to keep the nose up, since it tends to dip in a turn.

We've already discussed how stalls occur in a sailplane, and recovering from them is something a student practices again and again until it becomes a reflex action. Every plane acts differently as it approaches a stall, but nearly all give some warning. Most begin to vibrate and make moaning noises, and the controls move in a mushy manner. You'll become so familiar with these warnings that you will instinctively push the stick forward and keep the wings level when you feel or hear them. Recovering from stalls repeatedly in practice will give you confidence in yourself and in your sailplane. And knowledge of the plane's stall characteristics will aid you in staying above the minimum safe approach speed for landing.

Your instructor won't allow you to land the sailplane

during your early lessons, but he'll be explaining the procedure to you as he lands. You would do well to observe everything he does. He's been keeping an eye on the altimeter as you've been flying, and now he sees you have lost enough altitude so that you should go back to the field and land. Soaring pilots must always remember to head for the field while there is still sufficient altitude to make the normal landing approach in a pattern. The landing pattern is rectangular, and depending on the airport it may require left turns (called a left-hand approach) or the approach may be a right-hand one. Left-hand approaches are most commonly used.

The landing pattern has four legs, ending with the plane landing into the wind. The first leg is the direction in which the aircraft flies when it enters the pattern. Depending on the practice of the local gliderport, there are two methods of flying this leg. When it is called the *entry leg,* the sailplane flies in a direction that is a 45-degree angle to the runway (see diagram). At other fields pilots fly a *crosswind leg,* which means they fly in a path that crosses over the runway, then make a 90° turn onto the *downwind leg.* In either case, the sailplane usually enters the landing pattern at about 1,000 feet altitude over a prominent landmark, such as a building or a clump of trees, which is recognized by all the local pilots as the entry point.

As your instructor does this, he is glancing in all directions to make sure there are no other aircraft in the immediate area. He also looks at the wind sock on the field to be sure the wind hasn't changed direction and that he'll be landing into the wind. He has the sailplane's nose pointed down, to maintain the airspeed well above stalling speed and to lose altitude steadily for the landing approach. By the time he turns onto the *crosswind leg,* which runs parallel to the runway, the sailplane is down to about 600 or

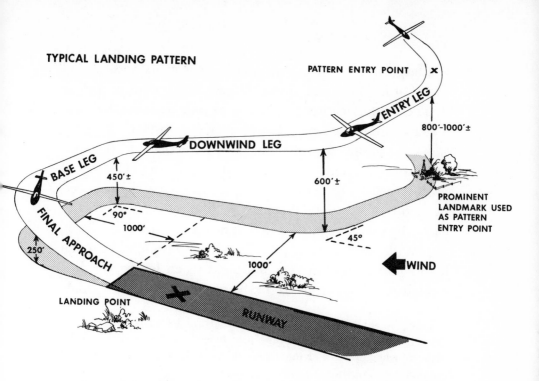

TYPICAL LANDING PATTERN

PATTERN ENTRY POINT

ENTRY LEG

800'-1000'±

DOWNWIND LEG

BASE LEG

450'±

600'±

PROMINENT
LANDMARK USED
AS PATTERN
ENTRY POINT

FINAL APPROACH

90°

1000'

45°

250'

1000'

WIND

LANDING POINT

RUNWAY

700 feet. If he isn't losing altitude fast enough, he pulls the lever which activates the spoilers on the wings. He's keeping an eye on both the altimeter and the airspeed indicator. You're coming down more rapidly now, and the planes, cars, and people on the field are looming larger.

By the time your plane continues past the end of the landing strip the altitude has been reduced to 400 to 500 feet and the spoilers are closed. Now the pilot makes a sharp, banking turn to the left and enters the *base leg*. This short leg barely allows enough time to level out the sailplane before another 90° turn to the left is made. Now you are on *final approach*, at about 200 to 300 feet, and he has leveled the wings quickly. This is the most critical leg, and the sailplane must have sufficient altitude to make it all the way to the landing strip and sufficient airspeed to avoid any danger of a stall. This is where beginning pilots have to overcome their natural instincts. Suppose the plane's approach is a little low. The landing strip is in sight, but there is a large tree or a fence looming larger every second and the pilot is concerned about the sailplane's ability to clear it. The beginner's first instinct is to pull back on the stick and lift the plane's nose to get over the obstacle. But this slows the airspeed, which causes a reduction in lift and a "mushing" descent, so the aircraft sinks faster. He should push forward a little on the stick and increase the airspeed by pointing the nose down. It will create extra lift and carry the sailplane farther so that he can clear the obstacle.

With experience a pilot learns to recognize how the landing strip looks in his windshield when his approach is too low, too high or just right. By memorizing this, he finds

A sailplane pilot must go against his natural instincts to gain distance in landing. Pulling the nose up causes loss of airspeed and the plane mushes down. Putting the nose down increases airspeed and the plane flies farther.

MUSHING DESCENT

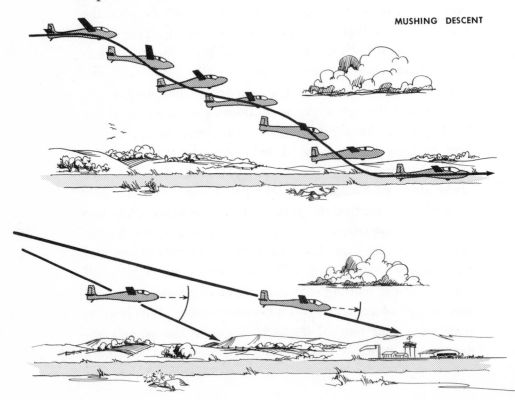

NOSE DOWN WILL CARRY YOU FARTHER

A sailplane pilot executes a "flare-out," leveling off for touchdown.

it easier to judge quickly and make the necessary corrections with his controls during final approach.

Your instructor seems to be making a very steep descent as the landing strip gets closer and closer. Just as you're beginning to wonder if the sailplane is going to land nose first, he pulls back abruptly on the stick. The plane levels out quickly and skims along a few feet above the ground for about 200 feet. He has executed his "flare-out" and the plane is now in perfect position for an easy landing.

 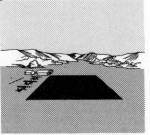 

TOO LOW   **CORRECT LANDING STRIP PERSPECTIVE**   TOO HIGH

A pilot learns to memorize how the landing strip looks in his windshield as he makes his landing approach.

He opens the spoilers again and the sailplane settles onto the ground with only the slightest bumping. After it rolls along the airstrip a short distance, the instructor applies the wheel brake. The aircraft skids to a stop quickly and the right wing tip drops to the ground. You've been too busy on this flight to marvel at the wonder of it all, but you'll remember it later.

4

Cross-country, Competition and Awards

The majority of soaring enthusiasts find their fun in local flying. They seek out the sources of lift and soar within gliding distance of the field, and they have the security of knowing they can go back to the gliderport and land if they run out of good lift.

Only the more experienced pilots are prepared for cross-country flights, which require careful planning, resourcefulness and more than adequate flying skills. Although flights of 700 miles have been made in sailplanes, the possibility of finding enough sources of lift all along the route of a long-distance flight is just that—a possibility. The most successful cross-country flights are a combination of good fortune in having sufficient lift available and the pilot's skill at navigating and taking advantage of lift. If the pilot fails to find sufficient lift to keep him going all the way to his goal, he'll have to land in a farmer's field or some other suitable place along the route. Then it will probably be necessary for his ground crew or some friends to help him disassemble the sailplane and tow it away on a

Cross-country flights require careful planning and resourcefulness.

trailer built especially for this purpose. (These aircraft are designed so that the wings and tail assembly may be quickly connected with or disconnected from the fuselage.)

When soaring pilots progress to the stage where they want to begin flying cross-country, they start with a fairly short trip. This experience usually gives them the ability to undertake increasingly longer flights. The first flight should probably be to a location not far away, and then a return to the starting field. Then the pilot can progress to longer one-way flights with landings at different fields. If the other field is an airport, he can arrange for the tow plane to fly there and tow his sailplane home. Or he may arrange to have his volunteer ground crew (which may consist of his wife, children, or friends) meet him there with a trailer.

Anyone who plans to do cross-country soaring should be prepared to make off-field landings—in other words, landings in places not designed for aircraft operations. If possible, he should practice some off-field landings with an instructor. It's necessary to judge from the air whether the field is sufficiently level, how bumpy the surface is, the wind direction (so he can land into the wind), and the height of any obstacles in the landing approach path.

A thorough briefing on the weather conditions enroute to the destination goal is required on the day of the flight. The pilot has to know what types of clouds, visibility, and winds he can expect and whether any precipitation or storms may rule out a soaring trip in that area.

Navigation and map reading ability is also critically important. A student pilot is required to have flight instruction in cross-country navigation before he is allowed to fly solo outside the local area designated by his flight instructor. He must demonstrate his knowledge of and ability to use aeronautical charts and the compass.

Most aeronautical maps are compiled by the U. S. Department of Commerce Coast and Geodetic Survey, and they're called "sectional charts." One inch on these charts equals about eight miles on the ground. Aeronautical maps are used just as road maps are, but in addition to rivers, roads, and railroads, they show terrain elevations and radio beams used by power planes for radio navigation. A good way to become familiar with the use of these maps is to ask a power-plane pilot (perhaps the tow-plane pilot) for a ride as a passenger when he's flying anywhere outside the immediate area of the gliderport. The student can study the map in flight and relate it to the ground area being flown over.

Flight instruction in navigation is required before students fly cross-country.

Pilots who fly frequent cross-country trips usually have their volunteer ground crews well-rehearsed and informed about the planned flight route and the corresponding ground routes leading to the destination. Most equip the sailplane and the car towing the trailer with two-way radios in order to maintain contact enroute. Then if the pilot is required to land short of his goal, he can help direct the ground crew to the area where he lands. Sometimes lift conditions will be better in a route that isn't a straight, direct path to the destination goal, and the pilot will change his route while in flight. The radio is especially useful in this situation.

Thermals are the most commonly used form of lift in

cross-country flying, although a pilot will take advantage of ridge lift, too, if he encounters it enroute. But the main part of the flight usually depends on thermal lift. The pilot finds a thermal, circles tightly in it and rises as high as he can go, then flies off to find the next thermal in the general direction of his goal. He hoards altitude and tries to plan ahead. He knows he is going to lose altitude after he leaves a thermal, but if he has gained enough in the thermal, he has extra altitude to "spend" while searching for the next lift. It's a fascinating game, and if he is resourceful and plans carefully to make the best use of lift and altitude, he can keep going on and on toward his destination goal.

The challenge of flying cross-country in a sailplane is satisfying in itself, but it can be even more fun if you're competing with other soaring enthusiasts to see who can fly the same route in the shortest time, or simply who can

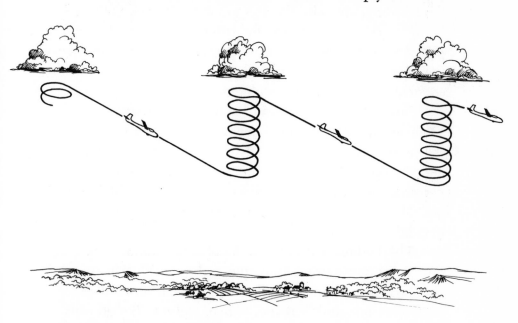

Cross-country soaring often consists of finding a thermal, rising in it, then moving on to find another.

fly the farthest. In fact, these are the two basic types of competition in soaring: competing against yourself to accomplish individual goals, and competing against other pilots to win contests.

Both types of competition have been formally organized by soaring enthusiasts to provide official recognition for achievements. The sport of soaring is organized on a worldwide basis, and the governing body is the Federation Aeronautique Internationale. Each country where soaring is organized has its own association, which is responsible to the FAI. In the United States it is the Soaring Society of America. The SSA administers awards for achievement in this country, and the rules and requirements for them are exactly the same as in other countries all over the world.

Beginning with the most basic achievements, the first three awards given by the SSA are the A, B, and C badges. Many of the requirements for these awards can be completed in flight training, and by the time a pilot has reached the stage where he is considered qualified to fly cross-country, he has usually completed them.

But it will take considerably more experience and achievement before a pilot can fulfill the requirements for the remaining awards: the Silver Badge, the Gold Badge, and the Gold Badge with three diamonds. Only a small percentage of soaring pilots have earned a Gold Badge, and an even smaller number the Gold Badge with diamonds.

The badges are actually lapel pins, standardized in design for recognition throughout the world. The pin is circular, with white sea gulls on a blue background. An A Badge has one gull, a B Badge two, and a C Badge three. The Silver Badge has a silver wreath surrounding the C Badge design, and the Gold Badge has a gold wreath. One, two, or three diamonds are added to designate these extra awards. Applicants for the awards must fill out an official SSA application form, listing their accomplishments and adding proof or certification by qualified SSA observers. Barograph readings are used as proof of altitude gain, and aerial photographs of designated points as proof of distance flown.

Here are the requirements for the A, B and C badges, as established under the SSA's ABC Training Program:

REQUIREMENT FOR THE A BADGE

Preflight phase

Applicant has knowledge of:

Glider nomenclature.

Glider handling procedures.

Glider preflight check.

Airport rules and Federal Aviation Regulations.

Tow equipment signals and procedures.

Hook-up of tow rope or cable.

Takeoff signals.

Pilot responsibilities.

Applicant holds:

Valid FAA student glider-pilot certificate.

Suitable log book.

Pre-solo phase

Applicant has completed the following minimum training program:

Familiarization flight.

Cockpit check procedure.

Effects of controls, on the ground and in flight.

Takeoff procedure, crosswind takeoffs.

Flight during tow.

Straight and level flight.

Simple turns.

Circuit procedure and landing patterns.

Landing procedure, downwind and crosswind landings.

Moderate and steep turns up to 720° in both directions.

Stalls and stall recovery.

Conditions of spin entry and spin recovery.

Effective use of spoilers/flaps and slips.

Emergency procedures.

Oral exam on Federal Aviation Regulations.

Solo flight.

REQUIREMENT FOR THE B BADGE

Practice phase

Demonstration of soaring ability by solo flight of at least 5 minutes' duration above point of release or starting point (low point after release), *or* 30 minutes' duration after release from 2,000-foot tow (add 1½ minutes/100 feet tow above 2,000 feet).

REQUIREMENT FOR THE C BADGE

Pre-cross-country phase

Dual soaring practice, including instruction in techniques for soaring thermals, ridges, and waves (simulated flight and/or ground instruction may be used when suitable conditions do not exist).

APPLICANT MUST HAVE KNOWLEDGE OF:

(a) Cross-country soaring procedure recommended in the *American Soaring Handbook.*

(b) Glider assembly, and retrieving.

(c) Dangers of cross-country flying.

Solo practice (two hours minimum).

Demonstration of ability to carry out simulated cross-country landing in restricted areas without reference to altimeter. Demonstration of soaring ability by solo flight of at least 30 minutes' duration above point of release or starting point (low point after release), *or* 60 minutes' duration after release from 2,000-foot tow (add 1½ minutes/100 feet tow above 2,000 feet).

The rules for qualification for the Silver Badge, the Gold Badge and the Gold Badge with diamonds are quite complex and specific about the way in which the requirements must be completed. A soaring pilot should study them before attempting to qualify. The *basic* requirements are:

Silver Badge
A duration flight of at least 5 hours.
A distance flight of at least 31.1 statute miles, made in a straight line.
An altitude flight with a gain in height of at least 3,281 feet.
Gold Badge
A duration flight of at least 5 hours (the same flight may count for both Silver and Gold badge duration requirement).
A distance flight of at least 186.4 statute miles made either:

(a) in a straight line; or
(b) around a triangular course; the turning points must be previously declared; or
(c) in a broken line of not more than two legs; the turning point must be previously declared; or
(d) out and return.
An altitude flight with a gain in height of at least 9,842 feet.

Gold Badge with Diamonds

The pilot is awarded a diamond to attach to his badge for *each* of the following three performances:

(1) A distance flight of at least 310.7 statute miles, made in either of the four methods described for the distance requirement for the Gold Badge.

(2) A flight made to a declared goal of at least 186.4 statute miles in either of the four methods described for the distance requirement for the Gold Badge.

(3) An altitude flight with a gain in height of at least 16,404 feet.

It's obvious that in competing with himself for increasingly challenging achievements, there is no lack of goals for the soaring pilot. Nor is there any lack of competition with others. There are many local meets, regattas and contests where you won't find yourself competing with Diamond Badge pilots flying expensive, high-performance planes. The SSA's *Soaring* magazine carries a calendar of them in every issue.

Local meets are informal, open-house, picnic-style gatherings where friends and relatives join the pilots for a weekend of fun. Many bring campers, trailers, tents, and sleeping bags and make it a weekend outing in the country. Those in charge of the meet set up relatively uncomplicated tasks within the general ability of every pilot. There are speed tasks in which each pilot flies to a goal and returns, or flies around a triangular course. Times are carefully noted and average speeds computed, and the fastest sailplane wins. Pilots must take a camera with them and photograph the designated turn points in flight to prove that they passed around them.

There are also distance tasks. In a free-distance task, a

pilot flies as far as possible from the field in any direction, and the one who flies the farthest wins. This type of competition depends on each pilot's crew being able to follow him with a trailer and tow the sailplane back to the site of the meet. Some distance tasks are out-and-return flights to pre-announced goals, which saves the crews from long-distance travel on the ground. Other distance tasks require flying within a confined area, between two turn points. The pilot who can fly back and forth between the two points for the longest total distance wins. The type of lift and the availability of it keep any of these meets from ever becoming routine. The challenge of staying aloft for sufficient lengths of time varies from one day to the next, and this is one of the things that keeps soaring interesting.

The SSA sanctions and regulates regional meets, which are more advanced in the tasks and the level of pilot competition. There is a point scoring system and trophies for the winning pilots. The pilots are also competing for a place in the national championship meet each year. Winners of the national meets are vying for membership in the United States team sponsored by the SSA to compete in the world championship meets held every two years.

Only pilots with the Silver Badge may compete in the regional event, and a Gold Badge is required for the national meet. But the vast majority of meets are local, planned for the fun of the average soaring enthusiast. Local meets are probably the best examples of what makes soaring such an enjoyable sport: the cheerfulness, the outdoor setting, the families and friends, the picnic food, and the swapping of stories over a campfire after a day of flying. More men and women every year are discovering the sheer joy, challenge, and excitement of this fast-growing sky sport.

PART II

HANG GLIDING

5

The Why and How of Hang Gliding

Hang gliding is such a new sport that many people aren't aware of what it is. Some have seen pictures or heard about enthusiasts who leap from the tops of sand dunes and hill slopes, suspended from kitelike contraptions. These activities don't appear to have much connection with aviation, yet there is a relationship stretching back more than eighty years to its pioneer roots.

Man's earliest knowledge about heavier-than-air flight was gained by experimenting with glider flights. Otto Lilienthal, the great German designer, made more than two thousand flights in various hang gliders he invented before 1900. His scientific observation and notes helped people understand the principles of flight. Adding to this knowledge were John Montgomery, Octave Chanute, and other pioneers who also designed gliders and experimented with them in the late 1800s. Orville and Wilbur Wright consulted with some of these other experts as they conducted their long series of experimental glider flights at Kitty Hawk, North Carolina. They advanced the science of aerodynamics by improving wing designs, among other things, on the way to their historic invention of powered aircraft. But the Wright brothers' 1903 triumph caused the virtual abandonment of experimental gliding as the world focussed its attention on powered flight.

It was nearly sixty years later that a small group of aviation enthusiasts began to look again at the low-speed, low-altitude aspects of flight. By this time technology had advanced powered aviation to a degree of refinement beyond the imagination of even the Wright brothers. Speed, power, and distance were everything. Supersonic planes had shattered one record after another, and sophisticated space vehicles were being designed to carry men to the moon. Indeed, there seemed to be few goals left to attain, especially for the individual aviator.

But there was one last aviation frontier, where an individual could find personal adventure and perhaps contribute to scientific knowledge. Ironically, man knows more about supersonic flight and travel in outer space than he does about the aerodynamics of low-speed, man-powered flight. Few engineers have a really detailed knowledge of what happens to an airfoil at twenty-five miles per hour. The sport of *soaring* has advanced and sailplanes have become more sophisticated, but they fly at faster speeds and can be understood in terms of traditional aviation principles. But what of the lower and slower form of gliding? The knowledge that Lilienthal, Chanute, and the Wright brothers had amassed simply stopped advancing when powered flight took over.

Now, hang gliding enthusiasts are exploring this neglected area of aviation, and they're doing it in the same way that the early pioneers did—by flying their experimental aircraft on a trial-and-error basis off sand dunes and hills. They have gone back to the writings of Lilienthal and others for knowledge, and they are adding to it. They have been helped by the availability of lighter and stronger materials with which to construct their aircraft, so their task is easier.

The hang glider enthusiasts a decade ago were mostly professional pilots and aircraft engineers who started tinkering with homemade glider designs on weekends. It soon became apparent that launching oneself from a sand dune in one of these small gliders was fun. Others took up the pursuit, and an exciting sport was born. In a few short years, it has blossomed into one of the faster-growing sports in the United States. Rapidly increasing thousands of people are taking an interest in it all over the country. It has a powerful appeal. It is the closest opportunity man has ever had to fly like a bird—not enclosed in a flying machine, but strictly under his own power. The majority of participants are younger people, because launching oneself and climbing back up slopes requires good physical condition. Hang glider flyers say the sheer exhilaration of this sport is unmatched.

The "hang" in hang glider doesn't mean that the pilot hangs from his hands or arms beneath the flying apparatus. It means that he is suspended below the wing surface on a swing seat or in a harness, either in a sitting or a prone position. Hang gliders have been defined as "aircraft in which the undercarriage and takeoff power are provided solely by the legs of the pilot." Technically, hang gliding also includes hang "soaring" since these gliders have the capability of gaining altitude and remaining aloft for long periods of time when sources of natural lift are present. Gliding means moving steadily downward through the air from a higher launching point to a lower landing spot. Soaring means gaining altitude when the glider takes advantage of rising air while in flight. Hang gliding is also

A hang glider pilot doesn't hang; he is suspended in a harness.

commonly called sky surfing and sky sailing when refer-
ring to the sport in general.

The aircraft on which this sport is based fall into two
broad categories: Rogallo wings and rigid wings. The Rogallo glider, a very light, easily portable, flexible wing concept, provided the breakthrough that made hang gliding
possible for masses of people. This triangular kite was developed by a space scientist, Francis M. Rogallo, and his
wife, Gertrude, in 1951. It was refined and tested exhaus-
tively by Rogallo for the National Aeronautics and Space
Administration as part of a research project aimed at re-
placing the parachutes that lower spacecraft to the earth's
surface after re-entry to the atmosphere. Conventional
parachutes didn't offer much maneuverability, and the Ro-

gallo kite could generate forward movement as well as lift. However, NASA decided against adopting the Rogallo device because it was difficult to stow.

People interested in aerodynamics saw possibilities in the kite as a glider, and it was soon being modified by a number of manufacturers as well as do-it-yourself builders. Today more than 90 per cent of the hang gliders being flown in this country are based on the original Rogallo design. They are made of various materials, but increasingly of aluminum tubing, steel cables and Dacron cloth. The metal tubing frame is laid out in the shape of the letter A, with a keel boom running straight back from the center point of the leading edge. The length of the keel and the leading edge tubes are usually the same: between 15 and 20 feet. The Dacron material stretched over this frame acts like a sail, filling with air to create lift. The whole assembly easily folds into a slim package for transporting on the roof of a car, and it only weighs from 30 to 50 pounds, depending on the modifications made for a particular model.

The Rogallo is the easiest hang glider to fly, and almost all beginners learn on it. The pilot runs into the wind to launch himself down a slope, and usually becomes airborne immediately. He controls the glider by shifting his weight, which moves the aircraft's center of gravity in the desired direction. When he wants to dive or gain forward speed, he pulls his body toward the rigid trapeze bar in front of him and his suspended harness swings forward. To slow the glider or raise the nose, he pushes back from this bar. To bank right or left, he shifts his weight in either direction desired. If he raises the nose too much and the wing stalls (stops creating lift) the Rogallo will usually fall gently like a parachute. You don't have to have an extensive knowledge of aerodynamics to fly this type of glider, which is one of the reasons for its wide popularity.

The Rogallo is the easiest type of hang glider to learn on.

Rigid-wing hang gliders are larger, heavier, and more complicated to fly than Rogallo types. There are both mono-wing and bi-wing designs, and some of them look remarkably like the ancient gliders flown by Chanute, Montgomery, and the Wright brothers. The Rogallo has a glide ratio of a little more than 4-to-1, which means it can travel a little more than 4 feet forward for every foot it descends in flight. Some of the rigid-wing gliders have glide ratios of 10-to-1, which means they're far more efficient in the air. Still, the Rogallos can often fly as high and stay in the air as long as the rigids when there is good lift to keep them up. Hang gliders have gained more than 1,800 feet of altitude in rising air, flown at altitudes much higher, and stayed in the air for more than 11 hours at a time. But the vast majority of hang glider enthusiasts limit their flying to heights of 20 to 50 feet and durations of less than a minute. Only the expert pilots with long experience should attempt high altitude flights.

There is no reason why hang gliding can't be a safe sport, and it *is* for those participants who use common sense. But the sport is so new that it hasn't developed to the point where it is as well organized as soaring. Carelessness and recklessness aren't tolerated by anybody in the sport of soaring, which has long had safety programs and formal training under the regulation of the Federal Aviation Administration. Hang gliding, on the other hand, is an unregulated sport, and there have been too many deaths and injuries due to carelessness. Most of the serious accidents have been caused by pilot error. Many hang glider pilots have been self-taught up until now, and some of these lack any training in safety procedures. Some refuse to wear helmets, even though it has been demonstrated that wearing one can provide excellent protection against head injuries in falls.

A leadership has emerged in the sport, made up of experienced pilots, hang glider manufacturers, and the organizers of meets. They are concerned about the safe and orderly development of the sport, and they would like to avoid public opposition and government intervention. The FAA's role is to protect the general public and air traffic, but so far it has regarded hang gliders as "momentary and brief users of the air" and hasn't felt the need to regulate the sport. Most hang gliders are not required to be certified for airworthiness by the FAA, as are other aircraft. However, this could change if hang gliding doesn't maintain a good safety record or poses what could be interpreted as hazards to the public on the ground.

Dick Eipper, president of Eipper-Formance Flight

Systems, one of the leading hang glider manufacturers, has said, "A lot of us are concerned about safety and how the FAA is going to react. One of the things we're doing is making aircraft-quality material available to people who build hang gliders. The manufacturers have an obligation to direct enthusiasts to build and fly their gliders in a safe manner."

Mike Markowski and Bob Goodness of Man-Flight Systems, a leading manufacturer in the East, stress safety both in the manufacture of their Rogallo-type Skysurfer Kite and in instruction to customers. Markowski, a former aerospace engineer for Douglas Aircraft, designed the glider with extra safety features to compensate for the failure of any key component. Both men have spent a lot of time teaching safety procedures in school programs.

The leading manufacturers have formed the Hang Glider Manufacturers Association to help influence the orderly development of the sport. Their avowed purpose is to impose a high standard of manufacturing and marketing, to insure a more standardized construction, and to become more responsible for the general safety of the consumer. They have established specifications for the materials and construction of the hang gliders they sell, and they require that an Association-approved booklet covering the basics of Rogallo flight be delivered with every glider.

Many manufacturers and dealers operate flight schools now, and these can be found in every part of the country. A beginner gains a big advantage with formal flight instruction—not only will he be a better pilot, but he'll learn safety procedures from experienced professionals.

The most experienced pilots in hang gliding have formed the Professional Flyers Association to use their knowledge in helping less-experienced pilots. Their aim is to help organize the sport along safer lines by sanctioning programs for the regulation of competition meets, establishing certification of hang gliding instructors, and working with the Hang Glider Manufacturers Association on uniform safety standards in hang glider design.

The United States Hang Gliding Association is the central organization in the sport. It is being developed in a manner similar to the Soaring Society of America, and is striving toward the point at which it will do as much for hang gliding as the SSA does for soaring. It will sanction local competition meets and act as a clearing house for information on all hang gliding clubs, organizations, and activities. It is already doing much of this. Now its officers are engaged in setting up a certification and awards program to recognize the proficiency of pilots as they gain experience, as the SSA does in soaring.

Developed with the help of the Professional Flyers Association, the program provides ratings in six different levels for pilots. The USHGA and the PFA can provide detailed information on the rating badges that can be earned, but briefly, the program works like this: Hang Badge #1 can be earned by beginners under the supervision of a rated instructor when they demonstrate adequate pilot control on several flights. The student must wear a helmet and keep a log book. Earning this badge entitles the pilot to practice on his own at a specified site.

Hang Badge #2 can be earned when the pilot has experienced at least ten flying days with a minimum of one flight per day in which he demonstrates good control and stand-up landings. Supervision by a rated instructor is recommended but not mandatory. More advanced flight skills will be practiced.

Hang Badge #3 requires a minimum of 30 flying days and at least 60 logged flights. A physical examination is required and the student must pass a written test. Advanced flight maneuvers, such as two 180° turns and stall recovery, must be demonstrated.

Before a pilot may attempt to qualify for Hang Badge ✻4 he must have had a level-3 rating for at least six months and logged a minimum of 5 hours actual gliding time. He is required to log 10 flights with 360° turns and one with a figure-8 pattern. He must demonstrate his flight skill before a qualified observer, and show knowledge of soaring techniques as well as gliding.

Requirements for Hang Badge ✻5 include passing a written examination designed by USHGA and the Red Cross Standard First Aid Program. The pilot must demonstrate mastery of all flight maneuvers under all flyable conditions and exercise expert judgment. Pilots with this rating are expected to be leaders and set examples of safety and skill to others. They will also serve as observers when other pilots are attempting to qualify for ratings.

Hang Badge ✻6 is the level for qualified instructors as determined by USHGA. At the time of this writing, the exact requirements were still being developed—with the greatest of care.

The responsible people in hang gliding are convinced that better organization and greater self-regulation will make hang gliding a safer sport and stave off government interference. Hang gliding is probably as safe as skiing, motorcycling, and some other sports, but *how* safe depends on the good judgment of the individual. If he's safety conscious, doesn't try to fly in bad wind conditions, and doesn't try to exceed the limits of his piloting ability, he stands an excellent chance of avoiding accidents.

It's a healthy, exciting, outdoor sport which offers exercise for both mind and body. And it offers a satisfying personal sense of achievement that is drawing thousands more people to it every year.

6

Getting into Hang Gliding

By the time you finish reading this book, you'll have a good idea of what hang gliding is all about. But you'll still be a novice, and if you decide you want to get into hang gliding, you should seek more information before devoting your time and money to the sport. You should start by writing to the Soaring Society of America (Box 6601, Los Angeles, California 90069) and requesting their information kit on hang gliding. It's free. At the same time, write to the U. S. Hang Gliding Association (Box 66306S, Los Angeles, California 90066) and ask them for information, including the local hang gliding clubs and dealers in your area. While you're at it, you should join USHGA and take advantage of a real bargain. Your $5.00 annual dues entitles you to a year's subscription to their monthly magazine, *Ground Skimmer*, which can help keep you abreast of developments.

Things are changing so quickly in hang gliding that it's necessary to read more than one publication to keep informed. Two other useful publications you can subscribe to are *Hang Glider* magazine ($5.00 a year), a handsome, color quarterly (246 North Fries, Wilmington, California 90731) and *Low & Slow* ($6.00 a year), a monthly (59

Dudley Avenue, Venice, California 90291). In addition, there are a number of local publications published by clubs, dealers, and manufacturers in various parts of the country. You'll find ads for them in the national publications.

The magazines contain information on competition meets, new glider designs, and flying techniques. The ads are also informative, showing the different models of hang gliders and extra equipment you can buy. Anyone who gets into hang gliding should also buy a copy of *Hang Gliding: The Basic Handbook of Skysurfing*, by Dan Poynter. This very detailed, technical handbook is the best reference book yet published on hang gliding. It includes charts and tables on the specifications of all the materials used in the construction of hang gliders as well as a complete listing of all models available. You can order it for $5.95 from Dan Poynter, 48–201 Walker Street, North Quincy, Massachusetts 02171. It's invaluable if you should decide to build your own glider, as some enthusiasts do.

Before you decide to invest in a hang glider of your own, you should become as familiar as possible with the various models being flown. You can start by reading the magazines and their ads, and then write to the manufacturers for brochures and other information. When you find a local hang gliding club, talk with the members and hear what they have to say about the pros and cons of each model. As a beginner, you'll want to concentrate on the Rogallo types. And it would be wise to limit your interest to those manufacturers who are members of the Hang Glider Manufacturers Association, since they are pledged to a high standard of materials and construction. A membership directory is included in the back of this book.

A question you may consider is: should you buy a hang glider (either ready-to-fly or a kit) or should you build your own? If you have a technical mind and are a good craftsman, you may be tempted to build your own from scratch. But it will mean you'll have to locate and buy all the materials from many different sources, and your skills may not include such things as cutting and sewing sails.

Unless you are exceptionally patient, hard-working, and motivated, you will probably be better off to buy a ready-to-construct kit (with most of the materials prefabricated) or a ready-to-fly glider. You can buy a good kit starting at about $300. Ready-to-fly aircraft usually cost between $500 and $700, for the best-quality models. You could build your own glider for considerably less than these prices, of course, but you may not save in the long run.

As a beginning pilot, you might not be able to tell the difference in performance between a Rogallo glider with an inefficient sail and one whose construction gives it better flight characteristics. But as you advance and gain experience as a pilot, you'll want the best possible performance from your aircraft. Sail stitching and cutting is a craft not quickly learned, and a professional sailmaker can do a better job than an amateur. You can see the difference in performance by watching a varied group of hang gliders fly. The smooth, quiet, well-fitted sails always outfly the gliders with noisy, flapping sails. If your homemade kite falls into the latter category, you'll soon become dissatisfied. Then you'll want to spend more money to buy the safe, well-designed, better-performing glider you could have bought in the first place.

It would be sensible to take flight instruction at a school or from a manufacturer or a dealer before finally deciding on the model you wish to buy. You'll be better qualified to choose the best model for your needs if you al-

Even youngsters can learn hang gliding, but formal lessons are recommended.

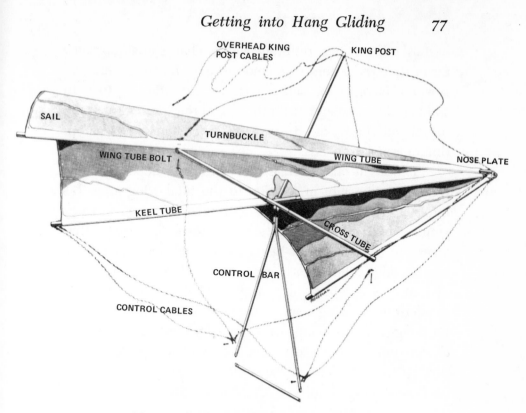

Main parts of a Rogallo-type hang glider.

ready have flying experience. If this isn't possible, at least try out some friends' gliders on the ground, running into the wind and getting the feel of them. If a formal flight instruction program isn't available in your area, you will probably have to learn to fly from members of a local hang gliding group or club. If the people who teach you are experienced, cautious, and safety-minded, you'll be able to learn the basics without danger. Then you can make the decisions about a glider of your own.

Individual manufacturers have added their own features to Rogallo-type gliders and so have owners in some cases, creating a variety of models. Nevertheless, they fall into four general categories: the standard Rogallo, the modified conical, the high aspect configuration, and the bastard. Each has different flight characteristics, some faster than the others, some more stable. But in general, all Rogallos have, as we said earlier, a glide ratio of 4-to-1. In still air, they descend at a rate of 400 feet per minute, and they fly at speeds of 18 to 25 miles per hour for their optimum cruising speeds.

The flight characteristics of a Rogallo depend on the weight of the pilot in relation to the total wing area. It's important to fly only a glider of the size designed to carry your weight. Manufacturers are careful to specify this. Sizes are usually stated in terms of keel length, and the leading edge tubes are as long as the keel. A Rogallo with a 16-foot keel is said to have a 16-foot wing. Another measurement is the wing span, and this is determined partly by the length of the wing's leading edge and partly by the *aspect ratio,* or angle at which the two leading edge tubes diverge from the nose at the center. Here is a general table for determining glider size for pilot weight:

Wing size (ft.)	16	17	18	20
Wing span (ft.)	20	21	22	25.75
Pilot weight	100–25	125–55	155–200	200–20

The standard Rogallo is virtually the same design from all reputable manufacturers. The sail fabric is almost universally Dacron today, and it is much better than plastics or other materials. The frame tubing should be aircraft-quality aluminum, and the fittings should be high-quality aircraft type. Aircraft-quality metal is higher stressed and much more exactingly manufactured than the metal parts you can buy in a hardware store.

The standard Rogallo is usually considered to be the safest and most stable hang glider, and the best to learn on. It is stable in a wider variety of wind conditions than many other types. It has a low flying speed, taking off at 15 miles per hour, and it can cruise nicely at 15 to 16 miles per hour, although it can be flown up to 45 miles per hour. It stalls at about 8 miles per hour.

More-advanced pilots sometimes like to fly the modified conical Rogallo, even though it is more difficult to control. The leading edges of the wing are slightly curved, which improves the glide angle a little and gives it a lower stalling speed.

The high-aspect Rogallo has an increased angle of the leading edges to the nose point and the length of the keel. This angle may range from 90° to more than 100°, lessening the sweep-back look of the wing. The result is better performance, but the wider wing is less stable and trickier to control. It's not the best glider for a beginner.

The bastard Rogallo is simply a hang glider that has been modified by its owner, who probably loves to experiment. Some owners change the airframe and add flaps, spoilers, and rudders. These changes don't always improve the performance or stability of the glider, and the owner sometimes risks his neck to find out.

The other category of hang gliders is the rigid wings. These monoplanes and biplanes are certainly more intriguing to look at, and their glide ratio is often 2½ times better than the Rogallos. But they are considerably more complicated, larger, heavier, and not as easy to maintain. They are simply more-advanced aircraft than the Rogallos, and a pilot can't lug one on his shoulder to a launching site and take off unassisted.

Some other differences: even the simplest design of rigid wing gliders has twice as many components as a Rogallo. You can build a Rogallo from a kit in from five to twenty hours with few tools. But the construction time for a rigid wing ranges from forty-five to two hundred hours, and there are some difficult requirements—particularly

More advanced pilots can fly the modified conical Rogallo types.

rigging the correct angles into the wings. In ground handling, one person is usually sufficient for a Rogallo, except in stronger winds when a second person may hold the nose down to keep the kite from overturning. With the rigids, two people are required in calm conditions and three or four when the wind is stronger. In launching, the pilot does it himself with a Rogallo, but one or two helpers are needed to balance the wings and the tail (if it has one) of the rigids. Control in flight is strictly by shifting pilot weight in a Rogallo. Pilot weight shifting is generally used to control the pitch (up and down movements of the nose and tail) in rigid-wing gliders, but a movable rudder (or rudders) controls the yaw movement (turning of the fuselage right and left) in combination with banking to produce a turn. In landing a Rogallo, the pilot can raise the nose for a "flare out" and settle down to land at zero speed with great accuracy. The rigid-wing craft usually land at speeds of 5 to 15 miles per hour.

The Rogallo has undeniable advantages in ease of transport, simplicity of construction, and ease of launching and flying. But the rigid-wing gliders, with their superior glide ratio and better overall performance, can glide better and soar better when the wind is providing updrafts, or thermals are providing lift. As a Rogallo pilot gains skill and experience, he may want to move up to flying a rigid-wing craft, even if it is less convenient.

The Quicksilver, sold by Eipper-Formance, is the most popular rigid-wing glider, and for good reason. It is the easiest rigid-wing craft to learn on when switching from a Rogallo since the pilot flies it in a similar manner—by shifting his weight and using the control bar. The rudder, which prevents the glider from yawing during turns, is connected by its control wires to the pilot's swing seat. The Quicksilver weighs only 53 pounds and is made

The simplicity of the Rogallo includes self-launching with no help.

of aluminum tubing, covered with Dacron. Its glide ratio is 8-to-1, it can be quickly assembled, and the pilot can launch it himself.

The Icarus flying wing is also popular. This strange-looking craft, a wing with rudders at each tip and on the tail, was designed by Taras Kiceniuk, Jr., a young man who has become one of the most famous names in hang gliding because of his remarkable flying skill as well as his designs. The two rudders create drag in their neutral position and give the craft more stability. They also provide more drag for help in turning and banking. They are controlled by the pilot with twist-handles. The flyer pushes against two parallel bars to make the glider go up or down or turn left or right. The Icarus is made of aluminum tubing, wood and styrofoam ribs, and a Dacron fabric cover. Like all Rogallos and the Quicksilver, it has a king post, a metal post extending vertically above the wing which anchors the wire braces that give the craft strength. There are both monoplane and biplane models of the Icarus. They can achieve a glide ratio of 10-to-1, depending upon the weight of the pilot. They are definitely not for inexperienced pilots.

A veteran aviator, Volmer Jensen, invented what is probably the most sophisticated high-performance glider in existence, the VJ 23 and VJ 24 "swingwing" monoplane. This 100-pound aircraft looks like some sort of pre-World War I airplane, and flying it is a far cry from piloting most hang gliders. Its controls are more like those of a conventional airplane: a control stick is used to activate the wing ailerons, which make the craft bank right or left, and the elevator in the tail, which makes the glider's nose go up or down. A foot bar controls the rudder, which is used to prevent yaw during turns, just as in a sailplane. These controls are located on the parallel bars beneath the wing. The

The Volmer Jensen swingwing is a very high-performance hang glider.

pilot literally hangs with his arms over these bars. There is a small set of wheels in front of the pilot, to cushion some of the shock in a hard landing. They are also useful in pulling the glider back up a slope after a flight. The wing, which has a plywood leading edge, is exceptionally strong and efficient in creating lift in forward movement. The VJ 23 and VJ 24 have a 9-to-1 glide ratio and can make tight turns without losing much altitude. They are FAA-licensed aircraft and only a pilot with considerable experience

should fly one. Volmer Aircraft also makes a high-performance biplane which is rated highly by enthusiasts.

Mike Markowski, of Man-Flight Systems, Worcester,
Massachusetts, has designed and built a high-performance
glider called the Eagle III, which has attracted considerable attention. The trailing edge of its 34-foot wing gives
it a batlike appearance. This aluminum and Dacron monoplane achieves a glide ratio of 10-to-1 and also has a control stick. But only the leading edge of the wing retains a
rigid shape; the trailing edge is attached to a cable that

Bi-plane hang gliders resemble craft flown by early aviation pioneers.

Mike Markowski of Man-Flight Systems designed the Eagle III with a "sail wing."

moves and changes the shape of the wing airfoil, depending on the angle that the glider is flying into the wind. This concept is called a "sail wing." When the wing stalls, it does so gently, settling downward like a parachute rather than going into a dive. Markowski considers the Eagle III a good high-performance glider for a Rogallo pilot to master.

There is a separate type of hang glider that looks like a Rogallo type, but is actually very different. This is the delta-winged tow kite introduced by an Australian, Bill Bennet, who performs remarkable stunts with it. Perhaps you've seen these kites on television. The pilot is towed by a speedboat or a car, wearing water skis or snow skis, and rises swiftly into the air. They depend on this outside power source for lift, and flying one can be highly dangerous except by an expert. A Rogallo-type glider could never stand the stress generated by the pull of the speedboat or car, and should never be towed in this manner.

Another type of tow kite, also built with superior strength, is the flat kite. This one will not glide to earth if its forward motion should stop; it falls straight down. It depends on the speed and pulling power of the boat or car for its lift. It is always flown at a carefully calculated nose-high angle, and its lift is generated by wind being deflected on its bottom surface.

Tow kites should never be flown by anyone who isn't an expert or who hasn't had professional instruction from an expert. If you think these are your thing, find an expert. Otherwise, stick to ordinary, man-powered hang gliders. There is enough excitement and sheer pleasure in hang gliding to satisfy anyone with a zest for an active, adventurous sport.

7

Flying the Hang Glider

It won't take you six months or a year to learn enough about hang gliding to be good at it. That's one of the joys of the sport. With a good instructor, you can take your first flight the same day you first pick up a hang glider—and you can do it with reasonable safety. The exhilaration of it will be so great that you'll want to fly again and again in a short time span, so you'll gain experience quickly. The key, of course, is safety consciousness and understanding of the forces that make your glider behave the way it does when you control it. A cardinal rule for beginners is: *Never fly higher than you're willing to fall.* Your early training should be on a gentle slope so that you're never more than a few feet off the ground.

As we said earlier, you'll become a better pilot and learn faster if you take flight instruction at a school. You can write or call the U. S. Hang Gliding Association and ask about the nearest school operated by a manufacturer, dealer, or flying club. The cost is very low and the course doesn't take long. If you can't do this, find the most experienced flyer in a local hang gliding group and ask him to teach you. If he has considerable experience, he's probably enthusiastic about teaching beginners. And he's probably safety-conscious. There's another rule: *There are old pilots and there are bold pilots; but there are no old and bold pilots.*

Schools and instructors may differ slightly in their teaching approaches, but basic training programs are pretty much the same. Most of them cover the material you need to know in this sequence:

Ground preparation
   Theory of flight
   Setting up the hang glider
   Preflight check
   Take down and neat wrap up of a Rogallo
   Transporting the hang glider
   Running with the hang glider
   Flare
   Right and left turns
First flight
   The harness
   Review of ground handling runs
   Basic rules of flight
   Launch
   Landing
Advanced maneuvers
   Coping with the wind
   Launch from higher up the hill
   Glide
   Turns
   Dive
   Specialized landings

You will be better prepared for hang glider flight instruction if you study and understand basic flight theory before you start training. The same aerodynamic principles explained in Part I of this book apply to hang gliders as well as sailplanes. You should read this section of Part I again. Briefly, we're talking about lift, drag, the angle of attack, pitch, roll, and yaw as they affect hang gliders.

When you pick up a floppy, lifeless Rogallo kite and run into the wind with it, it becomes an airfoil capable of flying. Air is forced over the nose plate at the center and all along the leading edge of the sail. The air splits into two parts, some going over the top of the wing surface and some going under the bottom. It meets again at the trailing edge. This is when our old friend, Bernoulli's principle, goes into action. Remember that the pressure of a gas or liquid decreases at the point where the speed increases. The air going over the curved top of the wing has to travel faster to catch up with that traveling under the wing, so the pressure decreases. The greater pressure under the wing forces it up, which creates lift for the glider.

In order for Bernoulli's principle to work, there must be forward motion. Thrust creates forward motion, and in this case the thrust is the pull of gravity on the hang glider. Starting from a launching point on a slope, the glider moves steadily downward through the air, going four feet forward for every foot it descends. It is usually cruising at about 18 to 20 miles per hour.

But there are forces that tend to slow the glider down, and these are called drag. The glider itself and the pilot suspended beneath it create drag as they push through the air, disturbing it. There is also drag created by the air spilling past the wing. If the angle of the wing is too high when it meets the air, the smooth flow of air over the top is disrupted and becomes turbulence at the trailing edge. This acts as drag, exerting a downward force on the wing.

The angle of attack is vitally important in flying a

hang glider, just as it is with all other winged aircraft. This is the angle at which the leading edge of the wing meets the air as it moves forward. The nose (and leading edge) of the hang glider is normally slightly elevated in flight. The air being deflected under the wing is generating lift, but the degree of elevation, or angle of attack, determines how much lift will be created in opposition to drag. When you raise the nose and increase the angle of attack, forward speed decreases. The degree to which you increase the angle of attack is important. If you increase it too much, the loss of forward speed eliminates the lift because air isn't being forced under the wing. Also, as we mentioned above, the air ceases to flow smoothly over the top and becomes turbulence, which acts in opposition to lift. If you increase the angle of attack enough, you will reach a point where the glider wing stops producing lift because the drag is stronger than the lift. This is called a stall, and the wing stops flying. Now the glider is just an object in the air, falling like any other object. Unless the pilot quickly changes the angle of attack so the wing can create lift again, the glider will crash to earth.

Every hang glider pilot has to learn to recognize the feel of the control bar at different angles of attack. It does feel different at each angle. When the nose of the craft is nearly level and the airspeed is increased, the force of the air on the glider gives the control bar more resistance. It feels stiffer to control. At a high angle of attack, the airspeed is slower and there is less air pressure on the bottom of the wing. As a result, the control bar feels weak and "mushy" when you manipulate it. With experience, you'll be able to judge the angle of attack by the way the control bar feels.

The natural forces of lift (rising air) that enable a sailplane to gain altitude were explained in Part I of this book. These same conditions apply to soaring (gaining altitude) or maintaining altitude in a hang glider. Hang glider pilots choose a hill or dune where there is a steady wind blowing against the slope. When wind strikes such a vertical obstacle, it moves upward and over it. By launching their kites into the wind on the side where it is striking the slope and bouncing upward, hang glider flyers find lift. Wind bouncing against a ridge provides ridge soaring, just as it does for sailplanes. Hang glider pilots can also find lift in thermals—columns of air that have been heated by sunlight reflected from the earth. This air is warmer than the air surrounding it, so it rises. Finding thermals is quite a challenge since they're invisible, but some of the clues and methods discussed in Part I can be applied to hang gliding.

Choosing a flying site is something that hang glider enthusiasts have to do carefully. In the first place, permission to fly may not be granted at many potential sites. One advantage of joining a local flying club is that the members have usually worked out satisfactory arrangements to fly at certain sites. Beginners should train on a gentle slope, starting near the bottom, when there is a *steady* breeze of 7 to 10 miles per hour blowing up the slope. Avoid trying to fly when the winds are gusty. Most hang gliders are unstable in gusts, because their control system—shifting the pilot's body weight—is unable to respond to gusts quickly enough to overcome their effect. If the winds are gusty, pack up your glider and wait for a better day. For about $5.00 you can buy a small wind meter at any hang glider dealer, and this is a good investment.

Make sure that the area of your intended flight path is not strewn with rocks or covered with trees. You're going to land there, and you're not sure exactly where. It should

An inexpensive wind meter is a good investment in flying safety.

be a landscape where you can fall a short distance without injuring yourself on sharp objects. Ski areas are increasingly popular with hang glider enthusiasts because they offer a cleared path, and the lifts can be used to transport pilots and Rogallo-type gliders back up the slopes. Sand dunes and beaches are favored, of course, because beaches are treeless and softer to land on than other terrain.

You should also avoid areas where the air is unstable. Vertical obstructions, such as trees, buildings, cliffs, and mountains, cause turbulent air pockets to form around the obstacle, and they are dangerous for an inexperienced flyer. Air spills over the top of the obstacle and forms a downdraft on the other side. When air strikes the face of a sheer cliff or steep sand dune, it tumbles in a turbulent pat-

Sand dunes and beaches are favorite learning sites when permits are available.

tern called a rotor, over the top of the cliff or dune. This force can cause a hang glider to crash.

It's a good idea to make a checklist of things to take to the flying site. If you have your own hang glider, be sure to bring all the parts and a set of wrenches the right size for all the nut and bolts. You should also have a roll of strong, high-quality repair tape for repairing minor tears in the sail that may occur. (If you should have more damage than that, do not fly the glider until it has been properly repaired.)

Hang gliding is a jeans-and-sweatshirt sport, but there are certain items of protective clothing that are necessary. First is a flying helmet that fits well. You'll see ads for these in hang gliding publications, and you can buy one at any dealer. Wear it at all times—even when you're handling the kite on the ground. It can save you some nasty head bumps and cuts. Sturdy gloves are also needed, because a pilot doesn't always land gracefully on his feet and gloves can protect your hands from bruises in a rough landing. Skiing or motorcycle gloves are good. Unless it's hot weather, a jacket or sweater is advisable—again, to protect you against scrapes or bruises in a rough landing. Rugged boots that cover the ankles are worn by many flyers. You'll be glad you have them if you land in a rocky area. Beginners are advised to buy a pair of knee protectors—similar to those worn in baseball or hockey—at a sporting goods store. Shin protectors are even better. Landings on the pilot's hands and knees are common among beginners.

It's a wise idea to bring a simple first aid kit when you go hang gliding, for treating minor scrapes and cuts. The type of automobile first aid kit sold by Johnson & Johnson is adequate.

If you or one of your fellow pilots has a small movie camera, you can take films of each other's flights. This can be a valuable teaching aid because you can view yourself in flight and evaluate your techniques. Hang gliding leaders also recommend that pilots keep a log book and note the date, time, place, wind, and weather conditions, number of flights flown and type of glider. You can also note your flying times and make comments on hard landings and stalls to review later.

One final thing on your check list: a trash bag in which to deposit cans, bottles, and litter from picnic lunches. Littering the flying site gives hang gliding a bad name and makes it more difficult to obtain permission to fly at sites. After all, hang gliding has been hailed as a clean, non-air-polluting sport. Littering the ground cancels out that claim.

One of the first things your instructor will encourage you to learn is a definite, orderly pattern of assembling your hang glider every time you fly. The manufacturer will provide an instruction booklet showing you each step to follow. You should never deviate from it, and you should practice assembling and disassembling the craft until you're thoroughly familiar with it. Why this emphasis? Because one bolt, cable, or wire incorrectly attached has the potential of causing the glider to crash. It's your life you're protecting.

The next step is the preflight check, and this should be conducted before *every flight,* for the reason we just cited. Mike Markowski of Man-Flight Systems has described the procedure in this way:

"When you have assembled the kite near the bottom of the slope, put it down with its nose in contact with the ground and pointed directly into the wind. Walk completely around the craft and check the integrity of all its metal components, making sure that they are attached properly and show no bends, breaks or cracks. Simultaneously check the fabric for holes, cracks or rips. Assure yourself that all points of attachment of the sail are sound and that no grommets have pulled away from the fabric. All rigging should be tight enough to twang when it is plucked."

Piloting a hang glider cannot be learned in dual instruction flights as other flying can, and you will make your first flight alone. But you can learn much about controlling the glider and become familiar with its response while still on the ground. You can learn how much to pull or push on the control bar to achieve the most efficient angle of attack, and how much to shift your weight to make proper turns. You'll gain a feel of the controls that will give you more confidence when you make your first flight.

Your instructor will aid you in these maneuvers, showing you what you're doing wrong and how to correct it.

He'll also introduce you to the harness in which you'll be suspended in flight. You probably won't use the swing-seat type—this is normally used only by experienced pilots, and it is not very safe for beginners. That leaves two harness types: prone and seated. Many pilots disagree over which type is the best, and it really boils down to a personal preference, based on the flying position the pilot feels most comfortable in. The prone harness offers the advantage of less drag in flight. But the beginning pilot will have more difficulty than an experienced one in rotating his feet down to the proper position in time for landing. If he's training in a beach area where there are no rocks or other rough terrain, he can afford to make a few learner's mistakes and end up landing on his face or stomach. If the terrain is rough, he'll be better off with the seated harness. Putting on the harness properly is essential, of course. All straps must be in the right position and secured tightly, and your instructor will stress practice in this.

You will try your ground practice without the harness at first, and then with it. Mike Markowski, who has trained many new pilots over several years, has explained the ground training procedures in this way:

"When you have inspected the glider, grasp the upright members of the control frame, lift the kit above you and run forward with the nose pointed directly into the wind. As you run, tip the nose alternately upward and downward at increasing angles to sense the effect. Raising the nose will cause the sail to inflate, catch more wind and pull upward, thereby reducing the speed at which you can run. Lowering the nose has the reverse effect; it decreases the wind resistance and enables you to run faster. Note, however, that lowering the nose excessively causes the sail to luff, with the result that the wind acts on the top of the fabric and pushes the craft down.

"Continue practicing on level ground until you can unerringly predict and 'feel' exactly how the wing will react to every angle at which you hold the kite. Then strap yourself into the harness. Continue practicing on level ground until the harness feels natural."

You should always keep the nose of the glider pointed into the wind, even on the ground. It makes it easier to handle, and prevents the wind from overturning the kite by hitting it at the wrong angle.

In practicing turns on the ground, the pilot grips the upper part of the control frame and keeps his elbows down. To turn toward the right, he moves the control bar to the left, easily and gently. Not much force is needed. To turn left, he eases the control bar to the right and the kite will pull around to the left. He should practice these maneuvers until they become second nature to him. He will also practice launch procedures until he's thoroughly familiar with them.

As we said in the beginning of this chapter, your first flight will very likely be on the same day that you start gound maneuvers, if you practice them thoroughly and feel ready to take the flight. Fear shouldn't play much of a part in this experience—you'll be flying at only a few feet off the ground, and you now understand the control of your kite and what makes it fly.

The most common error of beginners on launch is running too slowly and not fully committing oneself to the takeoff. It's called the "timid takeoff." It results in a stall and a slight fall because of insufficient speed to make the wing fly. Sometimes the stall is also caused by over-controlling the craft and increasing the angle of attack too much. Remember, with light winds you must generate the initial momentum to get the glider airborne, and you can only do this by running fast.

As you begin your takeoff run lift the glider until the

harness strap is tight as you gather speed. Shift your hands down to the bottom bar of the control frame, to give you easier control in raising the nose to the best angle of attack and keeping it there. Run hard and keep running—you have committed yourself and you're going all the way. Even when you feel you are about to lift off the ground, keep running until your feet no longer touch the ground. When you are airborne, tuck your feet up (you're on a gentle slope and the ground isn't going to fall away much) and keep the nose up, but don't raise it any further. It's easy to push too hard against the control bar at this point and stall the glider.

Your first flight will be a very short one, so prepare for your landing right away by lowering your feet for contact with the ground. You should execute the standard flare in landing. You do this by pushing on the control bar a few feet above the spot where you expect to land. This raises the nose, stops forward speed, and the glider settles gently to the ground like a parachute, at zero forward speed. The more you practice this maneuver, the more automatic it will become.

You'll want to practice these short flights over and over. As you gain experience the flight duration will get longer and you will have more confidence in your ability to control your glider. You'll have to practice keeping the wing level on takeoff and keeping the nose into the wind, and you'll learn on a trial-and-error basis. But take the time to thoroughly master the basic skills before attempting to launch from higher up on the slope. You'll be having fun while learning, so don't be in a hurry to expose yourself to greater risks by attempting flights at a level beyond your capabilities. Only you know the true level of your skills and confidence, so don't be influenced by other flyers who may be in a rush to move up to higher level flights.

When you are ready to move up to launching from

It's important to keep the wing level with the horizon, not the slope.

higher on the slope, be sure to check wind direction and speed carefully. You should test the wind characteristics by running down a short distance holding the glider overhead, without being connected to the harness. You're flying over a longer distance now, so remember to check the landing slope and be sure it is free of obstacles. If there are spectators in the landing area, wait for them to get out of the way before launching.

Remember that winds can change and they might not blow straight up the slope as you prepare to launch. If the wind is blowing at an angle, it may be necessary for you to launch into the wind at that angle, even though you aren't headed directly down the slope. It's important to keep the wing level with the horizon, rather than the hill. Don't follow the contour of the slope in your flight—keep the nose into the wind.

As you gain proficiency as a pilot you'll be ready to master some advanced maneuvers that are necessary for any higher-altitude flying. One of these is the straight glide. It sounds simple enough, but student pilots have a tendency to over-control their gliders, first pushing too hard on the control bar, then pulling in too much. The glider then flies in a wavy line, up and down. With experience, you will learn to use easy, gentle movements and to wait a moment for the glider to react to your weight shifts. At the slow speeds of hang gliders it takes longer for the glider to react to control movements than it does with regular aircraft.

Even though you have familiarized yourself with turn maneuvers on the ground, turning in the air is more difficult. It is necessary to increase your airspeed before banking into a turn, to prevent a stall. You should push the control bar gently and smoothly to the right or left, and it will take much practice to master this skill. Yet it is necessary if you want to fly along ridges, taking advantage of the ridge lift and turning to retrace your flight. It is also important on longer flights when you want to move out of wind that is moving in the wrong direction, and you may need it when making landing approaches.

For a little more help, study diagrams on following pages.

One maneuver a pilot with limited experience should not attempt is the 360° turn. It's an advanced maneuver, and it must be performed at a high altitude. The reason is that a considerable amount of altitude is lost in such a turn. The wind must also be steady, and a pilot should never attempt it near the slope or cliff from which he launched. As he comes around in the turn and is headed downwind, in the direction of the launch site, his airspeed may increase to the point where he is blown right into the launch site before he can turn away. The 360° turn requires precision control using the same techniques as in shorter turns.

Pilots learn to use easy, gentle movements on the hang glider controls.

It takes practice to learn to make smooth turns in the air.

The dive is another useful maneuver. It is used to increase the glider's airspeed, which can help penetrate strong headwinds. This requires a gentle touch on the control bar, too, for a smooth execution and recovery. The pilot pulls the control bar steadily toward him, as far as possible, to effect the dive.

More-advanced maneuvers include landing downwind, and crabbing into the wind for a crosswind landing. When a pilot has gradually advanced in his ability and mastered all these maneuvers, he may be ready for high-altitude flying. This is a different challenge from low-altitude

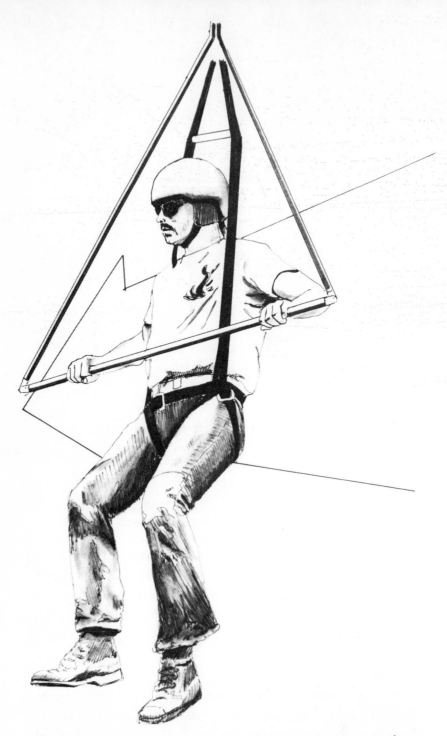

To increase your flying speed, pull your body to the bar. But if you pull too far, you will cause the hang glider to dive. Practice on gentle slopes will enable you to judge the difference between increasing your airspeed in this manner and causing a dive.

Hang glider pilots learn to land in a crosswind by "crabbing" the glider. With the wind from the pilot's left, he has positioned his body left and forward. This is to counter the tendency of the wind to lift the kite's nose and wing tip. He is also dropping from a prone position to have his legs ready for the flare-out and landing.

flying; it's no longer as easy to tell how fast you are flying because the ground isn't nearby as a reference. You might feel that your glider isn't moving forward much at all at a high altitude, when in reality it is cruising. In such a situation it would be a bad mistake to dive, thinking you were about to stall. You might not recover from a high-speed dive. But for those pilots who have gradually gained experience in a long series of flights from higher and higher launching points, high altitude flying can be the ultimate in hang gliding. Those who experience it say the sense of splendid isolation and freedom is mingled with a

Timid takeoffs don't work. You must run fast and launch yourself forcefully. With light winds, your legs must generate the initial momentum to get you airborne. The lift-off speed is critical in avoiding stalls in launching.

When landing mid-slope or when aborting a takeoff, keep on running after your feet touch the ground and slowly bring yourself to a stop. If you don't, the hang glider's momentum will pull you off your feet.

Move the control bar out slowly and gently when decreasing your airspeed or flaring out for a landing. Caution must be exercised to avoid over-controlling and stalling.

This pilot, who was flying in a prone position, has stalled his glider deliberately for a spot landing. Note the extreme forward position and how he has rotated his legs into position for the landing.

A normal rotation from prone position for landing is taking place here. The pilot's hands have moved up on the control bar, and he has extended his arms slightly for up control. This slowly flares the kite and decreases airspeed.

feeling of personal achievement unlike anything they have ever known.

Whatever the level of altitude in hang gliding, the sport does offer an excitement and enjoyment that would be hard to surpass. It is making personal flight possible to more people than ever before, at a cost that most people can afford. It is flying in the truest sense of the word.

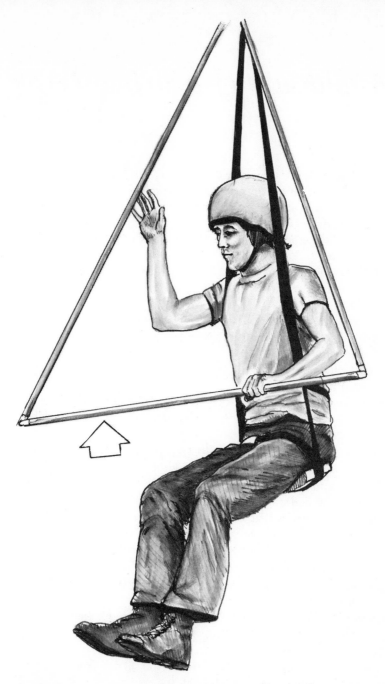

In the takeoff procedure, a pilot should always remember to move his hands from mid-bar to the bottom. The bottom bar provides greater leverage for all flight maneuvers.

A Glossary of Soaring Terms

Aileron—a panel in the trailing edge of an aircraft wing that moves on a hinge. It controls the roll, or banking, of the sailplane.

Airfoil—a wing or other surface shaped to create lift as it moves through the air.

Airspeed indicator—a cockpit instrument that registers speed through the air.

Altimeter—an instrument that shows an aircraft's height above the ground or sea level, depending on how it was set before take-off.

Altitude—height above sea level or the ground.

Angle of attack—the angle between the chord line of an airfoil and the relative wind.

Aspect ratio—ratio of the wing's span from tip to tip to the average width of the wing.

Attitude—the position or posture of a sailplane in the air, determined by how the aircraft is inclined about its vertical, lateral, and longitudinal axes.

Axis—a line that passes through a sailplane's center of gravity in any of the vertical, lateral, or longitudinal planes.

Bank—a sailplane's attitude when it rolls about the longitudinal axis and one wing is higher than the other.

Biplane—an aircraft that has two wings, one above the other.

Center of gravity—the center of weight of an aircraft.

Chord—the width of a wing section, measured from the leading edge to the trailing edge.

Crab—a movement whereby a sailplane goes sideward and forward through the air at the same time.

Control surface—the ailerons, rudder, and elevator that control the rolling, pitching and yawing of an airplane.

Dive—a steep forward descent.

Drag—a force opposite to the direction of flight, created by parts of the sailplane pushing through the air.

Elevator—a horizontal panel in the tail that moves on a hinge and causes an airplane's nose to raise or lower, thus changing the angle of attack.

Empennage—the entire tail assembly of a sailplane, including fin, horizontal stabilizer, rudder, and elevator.

Fin—the fixed vertical part of the tail, to which the rudder is attached.

Flare-out—a landing maneuver in which the pilot pulls the plane out of its descending attitude at the last moment and changes it to one that is parallel with the ground.

Fuselage—the body of a sailplane, as opposed to the wings.

Glide—moving forward and downward through the air, with gravity gradually pulling the aircraft to earth.

Glide ratio—the ratio of distance covered horizontally to height lost vertically. It is also called the ratio of lift to drag (L/D).

Hang glider—an ultralight glider, generally weighing from 30 to 100 pounds, from which the pilot hangs or is suspended, using his legs for takeoff and landing.

Leading edge—the front edge of the wing.

Log—a detailed record of each flight made by a pilot or an instructor. This is required by the Federal Aviation Administration.

Monoplane—an airplane with one wing.

Relative wind—the air that flows past the wing regardless of the attitude of the aircraft.

Ridge lift—lift that is generated by air rising up the side of a hill or ridge.

Rollout—the path of the sailplane on the ground, from the point where it touches down to the point where it stops.

Rudder—the movable panel connected to the vertical fin by a hinge.

Sailplane—any aircraft built to soar and glide.

Sink—an area where descending currents of air cause a sailplane to lose altitude at a faster rate than in still air.

Soar—to fly without losing altitude, and without an engine.

Span—the distance from one wing tip to the other.

Spoiler—a small panel which the pilot can raise out of the top of the wing. This disturbs the flow of air over the wing surface and decreases lift, making the sailplane descend faster.

Stabilizer—the fixed horizontal part of the tail, to which the elevator is attached by a hinge.

Stall—a condition when there is insufficient airspeed to generate lift, or enough lift to support a sailplane. The wing is no longer flying and the stall must be corrected by lowering the nose and regaining sufficient flying speed to create lift.

Stick—a vertical rod with a handle extending from the cockpit floor, used to move the ailerons and elevator.

Takeoff—the beginning of a flight.

Thermal lift—a mass of rising air generated by the heat of the sun reflecting off the earth.

Trailing edge—the rear edge of a wing.

Upcurrents—currents of rising air.

Variometer—a cockpit instrument that registers the rate of vertical speed of a sailplane.

Wake—the turbulent air trailing behind an aircraft.

Wave lift—lift generated by air rising within a mountain wave or lee wave.

Wing—an aircraft's supporting surface, in the form of an airfoil.

Wing loading—the total weight of a sailplane fully loaded, divided by the area of the main wing.

Yaw—a flat movement from side to side about the vertical axis.

Appendix

Hang Glider Manufacturers Association
Membership Directory (as of January 1975)

FULL MEMBERS

Up, Inc. (Ultralite Products)
137 Oregon Street
El Segundo, California 90245

Sun Sail Corp.
6753 E. 47th Avenue Drive
Denver, Colorado 80216

Manta Products
1647 E. 14th Street
Oakland, California 94606

Delta Wing Kites & Gliders, Inc.
P.O. Box 483
Van Nuys, California 91408

Sun Valley Kite School
17360 Beach Drive N.E.
Seattle, Washington 98155

Zephyr Aircraft, Inc.
25 Mill Street
Glastonbury, Connecticut 06066

Seagull Aircraft, Inc.
1554 Fifth Street
Santa Monica, California 90401

True Flight
1719 Hillsdale Avenue
San Jose, California 95124

Sunbird Gliders
1411 Chase Street No. 7
Canoga Park, California 91304

Hawk Industries
5111 Santa Fe Street
San Diego, California 92109

Free Flight Systems, Inc.
12424 Gladstone Avenue
Sylmar, California 91342

Chandelle Corporation
15955 West Fifth Avenue
Golden, Colorado 80401

Foot-launched Flyers
1411 Hyne
Brighton, Michigan 48116

J. L. Enterprises
1150 Old County Road
Belmont, California 94022

Sky Sport, Inc.
Box 441
Whitman, Massachusetts 02382

Eipper-Formance, Inc.
1840 Oak Street
Torrance, California 90501

Dyna-Soar, Inc.
3518 Cahuenga Boulevard West
Hollywood, California 90068

Man-Flight Systems, Inc.
P.O. Box 872
Worcester, Massachusetts 01613

Sport Kites, Inc.
1202 C. E. Walnut
Santa Ana, California 92704

Solo Flight
930 West Hoover Avenue
Orange, California 92667

Omega Hang Gliders
Box 1671
Santa Monica, California 90406

Kondor Kite Company
P.O. Box 603
Lewisville, Texas 75067

Muller Kites Ltd.
P.O. Box 4063, Postal Station C
Calgary, Alberta, Canada
T2T5M9

The Nest Airplane Works
1445-½ W. Eleventh Avenue
Eugene, Oregon 97402

Pliable Moose Delta Wing, Inc.
1382 Caddy Lane
Wichita, Kansas 67212

Apollo
722 Barrington Road
Streamwood, Illinois 60103

Chuck's Glider Supply
4200 Royalton Road
Brecksville, Ohio 44141

Sailbird Flying Machines
3123A N. El Paso
Colorado Springs, Colorado 80907

In addition to these full members of the HMA, there are many dealers throughout the country who are associate members. For more information, contact the U. S. Hang Gliding Association, Box 66306S, Los Angeles, California 90066.

Index